Attachment Styles

Practical Solutions to Transform Anxious, Avoidant, and Disorganized Behavior Patterns to Secure Lasting Relationships

Joyce T.

© Copyright 2023 - All rights reserved.

The content contained within this book may not be reproduced, duplicated or transmitted without direct written permission from the author or the publisher.

Under no circumstances will any blame or legal responsibility be held against the publisher, or author, for any damages, reparation, or monetary loss due to the information contained within this book, either directly or indirectly.

Legal Notice:

This book is copyright protected. It is only for personal use. You cannot amend, distribute, sell, use, quote or paraphrase any part, or the content within this book,

Disclaimer Notice:

Please note the information contained within this document is for educational and entertainment purposes only. All effort has been executed to present accurate, up to date, reliable, complete information. No warranties of any kind are declared or implied. Readers acknowledge that the author is not engaged in the rendering of legal, financial, medical or professional advice. The content within this book has been derived from various sources. Please consult a licensed professional before attempting any techniques outlined in this book.

By reading this document, the reader agrees that under no circumstances is the author responsible for any losses, direct or indirect, that are incurred as a result of the use of the information contained within this document, including, but not limited to, errors, omissions, or inaccuracies.

Table of Contents

Introduction 1
Chapter 1: Attachment Unveiled 6
    Attachment Styles 101 7
    Types Of Attachment 14
    Attachment And Adult Relationships 20
    Can Attachment Styles Change? 24
    Attachment Styles Quiz 27
Chapter 2: When Love Feels Like Chaos 32
    Characteristics Of Anxious Attachment 33
    The Anxious Partner In Relationships 44
Chapter 3: Thriving In Anxious Attachment Love 50
    Tips To Fix An Anxious Attachment Style (Or Cope With Anxious Attachment Triggers) 51
    Affirmations For Anxiously Attached People 56
    Mindfulness For Anxious Attachment 59
    Positive Reframing: Challenge Your Negative Thoughts 63
    Emotional Awareness And Regulation 69
    Setting Healthy Boundaries 76
    Relationship Strengthening Activities 81
Chapter 4: When Love Feels Elusive 84

Avoidant Attachment 101 85
The Avoidant Partner In Relationships 94
Chapter 5:Nurturing Love With Avoidant Healing 102
Benefits Of Healing Avoidant Attachment 103
Tips For Healing The Avoidant Attachment Style 106
On Deactivating Strategies 110
Avoidant Healing Strategy 1: Meditation 114
Avoidant Healing Strategy 2: Journaling 120
Avoidant Healing Strategy 3: Connection And Intimacy Building 127
Avoidant Healing Strategy 4: Challenging Negative Core Beliefs 130
Avoidant Healing Strategy 5: Improve Your Communication 134
Chapter 6:A Deep Dive Into Disorganized Attachment 140
Characteristics Of Disorganized Attachment Style 143
The Disorganized Partner In Relationships 147
Chapter 7:Finding Harmony In Disorganized Attachment 153
Practice Self-Compassion: Tame Your Inner Critic 156
Silencing A Harsh Inner Critic 164
Learn To Communicate Your Feelings 168
Activity: Self-Compassion Exercises 174
Chapter 8:Experiencing The Bliss Of Secure Love 176
Understanding The Secure Attachment Style 177
Communication For Secure Attachment 187
Problem-Solving Tactics 195

Nurturing Secure Attachment 199
Conclusion..205
References 210

Introduction

It is a wonderful evening—the sun has set, and you are out of work. You have time for whatever you would like to do tonight—self-care, relaxing while watching TV, or maybe even going to bed early to get some much-needed rest.

Except you are glued to your phone, doom scrolling through every social media app you have. Maybe you are waiting for a text message from your partner or boss, and you have convinced yourself that being on your phone will let you see it the moment it comes in.

Minutes turn into hours, and before you know it, it's a 3 a.m. stress-fest. Not only do you have to be up in a few hours, but you still haven't gotten that text.

Then there is the other side of the spectrum where you don't worry about those texts at all. During your wonderful evening, instead of reaching out to anyone at all, the first thing you do is turn your phone off. You don't intend to talk to anyone for the evening—or even the rest of the week if you have anything to do with it.

Every time you talk to someone, it somehow transforms into you getting hurt. After this happens over and over again, you can't help but feel that it's easier to be alone, to isolate yourself from everyone you know. That "You okay?" text goes unanswered for weeks. No one invites you to go anywhere anymore—everyone knows you will ignore the invite anyway. Your avoidance has left you utterly alone.

If you have picked up this book, then chances are that one of these scenarios sounds familiar to you. That nagging feeling of insecurity, the constant need for reassurance in our relationships, or the strong desire to avoid those relationships altogether to save ourselves from the pain and anguish.

What if I told you that there is a way to break free from this cycle? What if I told you that you never have to spend an evening hunched over a screen, willing a text to come through? Or that you never have to glance at a message and painfully turn the other cheek to keep yourself from getting hurt again?

In the pages of this very book, you'll discover the transformative power to overcome those anxious or avoidant patterns and build the lasting, secure relationships you've always craved.

You deserve better than allowing your past to predict your future time and time again.

Over the course of this book, you will master everything you need to develop trust, comfort, and happiness. You won't have to worry about those nagging "what if" questions in the back of your mind, nor will frustration over a mere text message seem like the end of the world. You'll never feel like you have to isolate yourself from potentially beautiful relationships ever again.

If this sounds like a dream, you're in the right place. This is the perfect time in your life to transform this dream into a reality.

You might be wondering who I am to guide you and why I'm best suited for the task. I, myself, have dealt with the pangs of insecure attachment for most of my life. That was before I understood the secrets to developing an attachment style that was truly secure. I've discovered the path that truly leads to secure attachment, and I'm here to share that path with you today.

Navigation Tips

Before we get started with Chapter 1, it's essential that you keep a few navigation tips in mind for the pages that follow:

- Before diving into the content, take some time to reflect on your personal relationship needs and challenges.

- Skim through the chapter titles and summaries to give you a sense of the book's organization and help you identify which chapters are most relevant to your situation.

- Read the book methodically, chapter by chapter, while taking notes or highlighting key points and actionable advice as you go along.

- After each chapter, take time to reflect on how the information relates to your own experiences. Consider how you can apply the solutions and tips provided to your specific relationship challenges.

- Make sure that you complete the interactive exercises and worksheets.

- As you progress through the book, develop an action plan based on the solutions and tips you've learned. Set realistic goals for improving your relationships and track your progress.

- While the book can provide valuable guidance, it's essential to recognize when your relationship challenges may require professional assistance. If you find that you're struggling significantly, consider seeking help from a therapist or counselor.

So, what are you waiting for? Hand in hand, let's get started on developing a new you that doesn't allow attachment styles to pick away at your time or comfort.

CHAPTER 1

Attachment Unveiled

Attachment is a unifying principle that reaches from the biological depths of our being to its furthest spiritual reaches. –Jeremy Holmes

Your attachment style plays a big role in your interactions with others, whether that be in the context of a romantic relationship or a platonic friendship. Embarking upon this journey of self-discovery and personal growth begins with a deep understanding of your own, personal attachment style. In this chapter, that's just what we'll do together—we will unearth how your attachment styles influence your behaviors, thoughts, emotions, and more in the context of relationships! Let's get started with understanding the elusive nature of attachment.

Attachment Styles 101

From a psychological standpoint, there are a few different definitions of what attachment truly is. However, we can simply define attachment by stating that attachment refers to the bond that a baby has with their caretaker(s) (Psychology Today, 2019). This attachment is how a helpless baby is able to have their needs met (or not met, depending on the attachment) by their caregiver. As a predominant psychological principle, it is necessary to delve into attachment style theory for an enhanced understanding of how attachment works.

Attachment Style Theory

Within psychology, attachment theory was developed by John Bowlby and expanded upon by other influential figures like Mary Ainsworth. The main focus of attachment theory as a concept is to explore the intricate interplay between our connections with others and how those connections form.

Typically, attachment is the result of how we develop in childhood and the relationship we share—or the lack thereof—with a caregiver. Although, it is certainly possible for attachment to be impacted by other influences throughout one's life span, as we will explore later on. Attachment theory also explores how attachments impact social and emotional development throughout one's life.

There are several key concepts that pertain to attachment theory, and understanding them will help you grasp how and why your particular attachment style exists in the way that it does. Those concepts include:

- Attachment: Attachment is, as I mentioned, the bond that a baby has with their caregiver. This caregiver is usually a mom or dad, but it can be anyone who is or was responsible for raising the child. This bond is crucial for the development of psychological and emotional well-being within a child and is intimately studied within the scope of attachment theory.

- Caregiver responsiveness: Also explored within attachment theory is how responsive a caregiver is to the needs of a child. This is a vital component of attachment and surrounds how sensitive and responsive a caregiver is to the physical, emotional, and psychological needs of a child.

- Internal working models: Attachment theory suggests that children develop internal working models or mental representations of how relationships work based on their early experiences with caregivers. These models influence their future relationships and interactions with others.

In essence, these key concepts refer to the connection between a caregiver and a baby based on the responsiveness to the needs of the infant and inform internal biases surrounding how relationships work for the rest of one's life.

Most professionals consider the existence of four attachment styles: disorganized, anxious, avoidant, and secure. Each attachment style comes with unique characteristics that will be explored throughout the course of this book, so do not worry about the differences between them just yet.

The Impact of Attachment

Why is attachment so important? What influence does attachment have on our lives and the world around us? Attachment theory says that the quality of our early attachments influences our emotional and social development. In other words, the way that we attach to people based on our childhood influences every single connection that we have for the rest of our lives. Because of this, understanding your attachment style is an infallible way to jump the hurdles posed by your individual attachment history.

One notable impact of attachment within our lives is emotional regulation. The attachment connections that we make as a result of our upbringing, therefore, influence how we are able to regulate our emotions, if we have that capacity at all! Emotional regulation refers to our ability to control emotions. For example, someone with strong emotional regulation can soothe their own anger without it spiraling out of control. This is intimately linked to improved self-esteem and resilience and is usually the result of a secure attachment style. This, then, implies that insecurely attached individuals struggle with emotional regulation.

Social relationships are also heavily impacted by our attachment style. Inherently, the way that you connect to other people influences those relationships, which is something to pay attention to when considering attachment styles and their implications. With a secure attachment style, you are more likely to have successful relationships that flourish and are built on the back of trust; on the other hand, those with insecure attachment styles struggle heavily with intimacy, trust, communication, and more.

Furthermore, your attachment style has a significant impact on your psychological well-being. This means that your attachment style can impact your mental health directly. You probably know the effects of this first-hand if you are someone who resonates with an insecure style of attachment; after all, the impacts are undeniable. To be more specific, however, those with insecure attachment are more prone to psychologically distressing disorders like depression and anxiety. In contrast, securely attached people are less likely to face negative mental health concerns.

In all, it goes without saying that your attachment style is certainly impactful across many areas of your life. When you are an insecurely attached person, social relationships, mental health, and emotional regulation pose significant concerns. The good news? These are all components of your attachment style that we will work on throughout the course of this book!

Continuity of Attachment

You should also be aware of something called the continuity of attachment when it comes to your particular attachment style. As you know by now, your attachment style and ability to attach in relationships is developed in infancy. This continues to influence your behaviors throughout your life, which can make it hard to overcome your attachment issues. At the same time, it is good to know that your attachment style is not deterministic. This means that your attachment style *can* change, and it does not have to negatively impact every single relationship that you have. This is something else that we will explore throughout the course of the book!

With this foundational knowledge of attachment theory, you are well on your way to further exploring how you can shift your attachment and succeed at doing so!

The History of Attachment

While the history of attachment theory is not necessarily instrumental to your journey, understanding that history can add a kick to your knowledge. Plus, it is really interesting to explore! Let's take a look at some of the major timeline points throughout the history of attachment:

- 1940s: John Bowlby began his early work. He was one of the pioneers of attachment theory, and his early work with children led him to question attachments. Psychoanalysts like Sigmund Freud inspired Bowlby's work, but Bowlby found the social and environmental factors to be more important than just what Freud and others studied.

- 1969–1980: Bowlby's groundbreaking work, Attachment and Loss, was published in three volumes from 1969 to 1980. These volumes are often considered the foundation of attachment theory. The first volume, *Attachment*, introduced the concept of attachment and highlighted its significance in early child development. The second volume, *Separation*, delved into the effects of separation from caregivers, particularly in institutional settings or during wartime. The third volume, *Loss*, explored the grief and mourning process, shedding light on how attachment and loss are interconnected throughout the lifespan.

- 1960s and '70s: Mary Ainsworth, a developmental psychologist and Bowlby's collaborator, conducted the famous "Strange Situation" experiment in the

1960s. This research aimed to empirically investigate attachment patterns in children. This led to the identification of attachment styles.

After these advancements, attachment theory continued to develop primarily from Bowlby's work. Contemporary research is developing every single day, which helps us make advancements in the world of attachment theory as well.

Types of Attachment

By now, you are aware of the fact that there are four distinct attachment styles. But why does understanding your attachment style matter in the first place? What is the benefit of doing so? Let's talk about it.

Why Should You Know Your Attachment Style?

There are numerous good reasons for understanding your attachment type, all of which help with personal growth, self-awareness, and improving relationships. When you take a look at the benefits of knowing your attachment style, it becomes abundantly apparent why such a thing matters.

For example, one of the benefits of understanding your attachment style is enhanced self-awareness. By definition, understanding how you attach to other people makes you more aware of your motivations, behaviors, interactions, and more. This can help spur positive change and growth—understanding what you do and why you do it allows you to correct those behaviors.

Beyond that, understanding your attachment style provides you with invaluable relationship insights. When you have a keen eye on your attachment style, there is much to be revealed about the tendencies that you exhibit in a relationship. For example, understanding insecure attachment might help you unveil why you feel distance in relationships. Through your awareness of your attachment style, you can work to eliminate certain attachment difficulties.

Communication skills can also be harnessed when you recognize your attachment style. Those with insecure attachment styles are prone to less effective communication, which can make it hard for your needs to be handled effectively. What's more is that when you do not understand your attachment style, you cannot communicate your struggles to others. However, when you learn more about your attachment style, you develop communication skills and conflict-resolution strategies that are unwavering.

Finally, having a firm grasp on your attachment style means that you can parent without allowing your childhood and past relationship struggles to interfere. This ultimately allows you to break the cycle of trauma and insecure attachment that may linger in your family, which in turn can help your child(ren) develop more secure attachment styles.

In all, you have to understand your attachment style because it is the key that unlocks enhanced interactions between yourself and others. This means that your attachment style can improve your relationships, both present and future, as well as how you feel within those relationships.

The Four Types of Attachment

For a lot of people, it can be easy to group attachment into two categories: secure and insecure. But attachment is a little more nuanced than that. There are four different attachment styles, and secure only makes up one of those styles, while insecure attachment represents not one, not two, but *three* other forms of attachment.

- Secure attachment involves being comfortable with intimacy within relationships. You feel confident that your needs will be met and form emotionally trusting relationships with those around you.

- Avoidant attachment involves minimizing how important emotional intimacy is. Someone with this attachment style will struggle to rely on others or express emotions, which means that trust is rare and vulnerability can be terrifying.

- Anxious attachment occurs when someone does desire to have strong, intimate relationships, yet they have a lingering fear of abandonment that impacts their relationship. This may result in jealousy, clingy behavior, and more—all of which can damage relationships.

- Finally, there is the disorganized attachment style. This style is usually characterized by erratic behavior, blending both anxious and avoidant attachment. Unresolved trauma or loss can show up in relationships, making them rather chaotic.

Throughout the course of this book, we will explore each attachment style in depth. Because each style is idiosyncratic and impactful, you will need to understand these intricacies and how they affect you.

How Attachment Styles Form

Each attachment style has different qualities and characteristics. One of the reasons for this is that each attachment style actually begins from a different place. While all attachment styles form as a result of how we connect with our caregivers in childhood, different childhood experiences lead to different attachment styles.

For example, those with secure attachment styles grew up with caregivers who were responsive and emotionally available. Secure attachment styles form when a child feels that they can comfortably explore the world around them and that a caregiver will be ready to fulfill any needs that arise. These children are well cared for and do not want for much, with all basic necessities being fulfilled.

However, avoidant attachment means that one had a different experience in childhood. They likely had parents or caregivers who were not emotionally available or were inconsistent, being caring one moment and then rejecting or neglectful the next. This prompted one to learn to be self-reliant and self-soothe from an early age, learning that their caregivers could not be trusted for emotional support. Such an experience creates avoidant attachment styles.

Then, there is the anxious attachment style. Anxious attachment stems from caregivers who were not responsive to their child and their needs. Neglect and inconsistency led to conflicting beliefs about how available caregivers were to support needs, which created anxiety and uncertainty about connection with others.

Lastly, we have disorganized attachment. People who grow up with disorganized attachment styles were raised by unpredictable caregivers who were even a bit frightening in how they interacted. Conflicting emotions and inconsistency paired with unreliability and fear result in a child who doesn't feel safe or supported by their caregiver.

Out of the four attachment styles, everyone falls into one. This means that not only can you not be without an attachment style, but your attachment style is certainly one of the above. If you are not certain of which one it is, do not worry! There is a quiz at the end of this chapter that will help you hammer out the details.

Attachment and Adult Relationships

Your attachment style is inherently impactful toward the relationships that you have in adulthood. From friendships to romantic relationships, you will notice how your attachment style impacts your ability to connect, communicate, and interact with those around you. However, this impact might not always be apparent, which is why we have to talk about the role attachment plays in selecting partners and adult relationships.

How Attachment Plays a Role in Selecting Partners

Attachment styles are very important when it comes to how people select their partners and then relate to said partners. We are influenced by preference, behavior, and dynamics, all as a result of our attachment style. This influence shows up in more ways than one.

For instance, attachment styles can influence compatibility. Most people naturally seek out partners who have a similar, complementary, or compatible attachment style to their own. Securely attached people often seek out other securely attached individuals, but anxiously attached people will seek out those who are anxious. This can reinforce dynamics and cycles, making it rather difficult for yourself and your partner to find a healthy balance when it comes to attachment.

Another way that attachment impacts relationships is based on who you select in order to repeat familiar patterns. For example, if you grew up with caregivers who facilitated your avoidant attachment style, then you are likely going to attract or seek out partners who behave in a similar way to your caregivers—providing you with inconsistent support patterned by bouts of caring only to be replaced with neglect. While familiar because of childhood, this selection only reinforces negative treatment and habits.

In addition, your attachment style plays a role in your ability to handle conflict. When securely attached, you can communicate in a healthy way that is conducive to problem-solving. However, insecurely attached individuals often struggle with trust, emotional regulation, and effective conflict resolution. This can impact partner selection and enforce the above, where you select partners who reinforce negative habits.

As a result of the above influences, it can be hard to attain relationship satisfaction. Securely attached partners feel far more satisfied in relationships, which is because they have the skills necessary to manage conflict and problems that arise. When one or both partners are insecurely attached, however, it is impossibly hard to find satisfaction within a relationship. This means that more conflict is on the horizon.

And in the midst of all of this, the attachment style you have and how it impacts your relationships can be one of the biggest barriers to growth that you face. Insecure attachment and reinforced cycles of toxic behavior can make it impossible to flourish, change your attachment style, or heal from childhood traumas.

Impacts of Attachment on Adult Relationships

Above, I mentioned many of the ways in which attachment can impact adult relationships, but let's dive into it a little further. Your attachment can impact adult relationships in innumerable ways, including but not limited to

- Communication and emotional expression. Insecure attachment can cause difficulty expressing emotions and opening up, or the opposite—oversharing and seeking constant reassurance. As a result, problems are not as easily solved, and there is a lot of misunderstanding between couples when even just one partner is insecurely attached.

- Trust and intimacy. Trust and intimacy serve as the foundational building blocks of a strong relationship, but those with insecure attachment styles can struggle with trust, either seeking too much reassurance or completely distrusting their partner. This, in turn, can make their partner feel like they have done something wrong to foster such a dynamic.

- Conflict resolution. Someone who is not securely attached can escalate conflict or avoid coming to productive solutions altogether. This can put undue pressure on a securely attached partner, as well as result in overall dissatisfaction for both partners.

- Parenting styles. The way you attach impacts how you parent, which can also lead to inconsistent caregiving when it comes to raising your own child. Not only can this cause your child to struggle with attachment, but it can also cause conflict between yourself and the other parent.

Your attachment style is one of the biggest and most significant influences on your adult relationships, no matter the caliber. If you did not see this impact before, then you certainly do now—and you are probably wondering what can be done to change your attachment style, and if you can change it in the first place.

Can Attachment Styles Change?

Many people are concerned with whether or not their attachment style can change, especially considering that their attachment style is deeply rooted in childhood experiences. For most people, it feels immediately like transforming one's attachment style is a lost cause, but this is not the case at all.

The fact of the matter is that most people *do not* change their attachment style, but that's not because it is impossible. When someone is unaware that attachment styles exist in the first place, or if they feel like they cannot do anything to change their attachment style, it becomes all but impossible to transform insecure attachment into secure attachment. However, this experience is not the rule—you *can* change your attachment style.

I mentioned earlier that attachment styles are primarily formed in childhood. They are formed as a result of their experiences with caregivers, and those early relationships impact how they think about the world around them. For most people, attachment styles remain consistent throughout adulthood—they do not just change of their own accord. It requires strong effort and dedication to change one's attachment style, which is something that you are going to work on in the coming chapters.

One way that attachment styles can be shaped is through therapeutic intervention, whether that is done with a professional or in a self-guided setting. Therapeutic tactics can help modify attachment patterns by allowing you to understand your attachment history. As a result, this helps you understand unhealthy patterns with which you engage and provides you with a safe environment to explore attachment issues. Over time, this can result in developing more security within your attachment.

Positive relationships with others can also contribute to the development of a more secure attachment style. If you only date people, for example, who have avoidant attachment styles, then you are not going to receive the support and care that you truly need to foster a strong, secure attachment style. But if you spend time in romantic relationships with those who are securely attached, not only do you get the support that you need, but you have a wonderful model for how attachment *should* operate between adults in a relationship.

Another tool that can help you shape your attachment style into one that is healthier is self-awareness. Self-awareness involves being familiar with your motivations and perceptions, including *why* those motivations and perceptions exist. This is one of the biggest reasons that people struggle to overcome their attachment plights—they do not know what their attachment style is, and they lack the self-awareness to dive into the matter with more intricacy. With tools and guidance to develop self-awareness, you can successfully overcome attachment struggles.

At the end of the day, you *can* change your attachment style; it is by no means impossible, and this book is full of tools and resources that will help you turn your attachment struggles into your very own superpower.

Attachment Styles Quiz

The following is a quiz that can help you identify your attachment style, or at least get a few steps closer to identifying your attachment style. For each style, answer the questions and score your points. Each response is scored as follows:

- (a) Strongly Agree: 2 points
- (b) Agree: 1 point
- (c) Disagree: 0 points
- (d) Strongly Disagree: 0 points

Here are the questions for the quiz, which you should score based on the guidance above:

- Secure attachment:

    I feel comfortable getting close to others.

    a) Strongly Agree

    b) Agree

    c) Disagree

    d) Strongly Disagree

I trust that my needs will be met in my relationships.

    a) Strongly Agree

    b) Agree

    c) Disagree

    d) Strongly Disagree

- Avoidant attachment:

    I prefer not to rely on others for emotional support.

        a) Strongly Agree

        b) Agree

        c) Disagree

        d) Strongly Disagree

    I find it easy to keep my emotions to myself.

        a) Strongly Agree

        b) Agree

        c) Disagree

        d) Strongly Disagree

- Anxious attachment:

    I worry about my partner leaving me.

    a. Strongly Agree

    b. Agree

    c. Disagree

    d. Strongly Disagree

    I often need reassurance of my partner's love and commitment.

    a. Strongly Agree

    b. Agree

    c. Disagree

    d. Strongly Disagree

- Disorganized attachment:

    I sometimes have unpredictable reactions in my relationships.

    a. Strongly Agree

    b. Agree

c. Disagree

   d. Strongly Disagree

- I have had experiences in my past that make it difficult for me to trust in close relationships.

   a) Strongly Agree

   b) Agree

   c) Disagree

   d) Strongly Disagree

The style for which you have the most points it likely your attachment style. Also, if you have the same points for avoidant and anxious, then your style is disorganized! Remember, this quiz isn't an official diagnostic guide; please seek a professional opinion if needed.

We have laid the foundation for deeper exploration and transformation. With this newfound awareness of your attachment style, you are on the path to building more secure, fulfilling relationships. Now, it is time to delve even further into the specifics. In the following chapter, we will delve into the world of anxious attachment. If you have ever felt that your desire for closeness sometimes transforms into anxiety or insecurity in your relationships, you are not alone.

CHAPTER 2

When Love Feels Like Chaos

Self-awareness is the ability to take an honest look at your life without any attachment to it being right or wrong, good or bad. –Debbie Ford

∞

The first attachment style that we are going to explore in depth is the anxious attachment style. As with each attachment style, those who are anxiously attached suffer from unique challenges that need to be faced. Not only are we going to explore said challenges, but you will be provided with practical, evidence-based solutions to turn your challenges into strengths. By the end of the next chapter, you will be armed with actionable strategies to navigate the world of anxious attachment and pave the way for more secure, lasting relationships. So, let's dive in and uncover the keys to unlocking a more confident and secure you.

Characteristics of Anxious Attachment

Overcoming anxious attachment begins with explorations of its characteristics. In other words, you have to know what something looks like in order to come up with solutions for it. Let's spend some time exploring the ins and outs of anxious attachment, including what signs you might notice in your own life.

Signs of Anxious Attachment

Anxious attachment can look a bit different for everyone who deals with it, but there are a few symptoms that are common to the attachment style almost unequivocally. For example, a hallmark of the anxious attachment style is insecurity in relationships. This can manifest in a few different ways.

If you are anxiously attached, then chances are that you keep a close eye on your partner's behavior. Without them giving you a reason to feel this way, you feel as though you have to watch out in case they are mad at you or are disinterested in your relationship. Often, those with an anxious attachment style feel the need to constantly ask for reassurance, which can be overwhelming for one's partner.

Another common sign of anxious attachment within a relationship is clingy or possessive behavior. Due to insecure attachments in childhood, it can be easy for one to feel as though they have to cling to a partner to prevent them from leaving—which, unfortunately, often has the opposite result of causing someone to be pushed away. This can often be coupled with jealousy; someone looking at, speaking to, or otherwise engaging with your partner can cause you to feel a fire of jealousy mount within you.

In addition, those who are anxiously attached have a massive fear of rejection in relationships. Fear of rejection can prompt you to try and please others in order to avoid perceived abandonment. This often compromises one's own boundaries, goals, and needs in order to find approval in the words of others, which can even cause you to *resent* the very person you hope to keep close to, as this people-pleasing habit is often one-sided.

Beyond that, one can suffer from a very high level of distrust due to this form of attachment. As a child, you may have dealt with a parent or caregiver who was very inconsistent, supporting you one moment only to leave you to your own devices in the next. This, in turn, leads to the deep-rooted feeling that no one can be trusted because of the expectation they, too, will behave in such an inconsistent way.

People who suffer from an anxious attachment style usually also suffer from a dichotomy of longing for intimacy yet feeling overwhelmed by it. Craving intimacy stems from a lack of it earlier in life; as a result, you may find yourself wanting intimate relationships and closeness. But at the same time, you are not used to such a thing, which can make that intimacy feel very overwhelming if and when you finally receive it. This certainly puts a strain on adult relationships of all kinds.

All of these combined difficulties can compound and result in low self-esteem and low self-worth, which only serves to cause more issues with intimacy, trust, and forming healthy relationships. Those who attach to others anxiously feel as though their doubts and unmet needs are a reflection of themselves and their quality as a person, which is not the case at all, even if it is a hard pill to swallow.

What Triggers Anxious Attachment?

For the most part, anxious attachment is not something that looms over your life every second of the day; it is something that has to be triggered to truly rear its head in your life. As it turns out, there are a number of different emotional triggers that can cause the symptoms of your anxious attachment style to show up.

For example, hot-and-cold behavior from your partner, where your partner is inconsistent in their behavior and actions toward you, can be a major trigger for anxious attachment. This is because such on-and-off actions can, whether intentionally or not, result in feeling much like you did when you were a child and dealt with an inconsistent caregiver. Even if you rationally know your partner isn't doing anything to you, inconsistent actions can trigger an uncontrollable swell of anxiety, fear of abandonment, and more—all of which heighten the signs of anxious attachment.

Something else that tends to set those with anxious attachment off is when their partner doesn't respond or takes too long to respond. Think about texting: If waiting hours between texts, even on occasion, is a massive emotional debacle for you, then that's definitely one of your triggers. While people with secure attachment recognize that things come up and cellphones aren't always accessible, the anxiety of someone who is anxiously attached can overpower even the most flawless rationale.

Additionally, avoidant behavior from a partner can trigger anxious attachment symptoms. Avoidant behaviors might seem like an obvious trigger, but many people overlook it. Being rejected in a physical sense, having communication attempts drowned out, or even having your partner walk away from you physically can send you into a spiral characterized by worry and fear of rejection. As a result, other signs of anxious attachment—like jealousy or clingy behavior—can become exacerbated.

Even more subtle signs of perceived avoidance or rejection can trigger feelings of anxiety for someone with an anxious attachment style. For instance, if your partner is spending more time than usual with a friend—or more time with a friend than they are spending with you—it can incite feelings of not being good enough, thus triggering other attachment-related symptoms.

That's not even the start of the triggers that can prompt anxious attachment to come out and play. Some of the other common emotional triggers that you may experience include

- Emotional distress. Feeling emotionally distressed, even if it has nothing to do with one's partner, can provoke emotions that do impact a relationship. For example, a bad day at work can turn into feeling like *everything* is going poorly.

- Criticism. Feeling criticized can be enough to spark feelings of inadequacy, which then prompt anxious attachment symptoms.

- Loneliness. Even if someone isolates themselves, the simple feeling of being alone can trigger anxiety or anxious attachment symptoms. One can feel isolated and, therefore, feel like they are not worth being around in the first place, for example.

- Perceiving a response to be cold. Whether verbally or digitally, a response that feels cold or uncaring can feel similar to the wavering care from a caregiver in childhood.

- A distant or distracted partner. Whether the distance has anything to do with them, an anxiously attached individual will perceive distance as an indicator of something negative—such as that someone is considering leaving them.

- Someone forgot an important event. If someone close forgets a birthday, anniversary, or another personally important event, that can be a massive trigger as well.

- Lack of punctuality. When people show up late to dates, events, or other matters that seem important, this can be something else that prompts anxious attachment symptoms to arise.

- A partner not noticing something new. Whether it be a haircut, a new dress, or anything like that, oblivious partners can be triggering too.

And the unfortunate news is that emotional triggers are not usually something that we can control. Because they are heavily dependent on the people around us, emotional triggers are inevitable; it is up to us as individuals to develop coping mechanisms that fight off those triggers and how they influence us.

Thought Patterns and Traps

Not all anxious attachment behaviors are started as a result of triggers; sometimes, these behaviors fester as a result of thought patterns and traps, formally referred to as cognitive distortions. Cognitive distortions are, as the name would suggest, distorted patterns of thinking that are not truthfully representative of reality.

Sometimes, these distorted thoughts can become our primary motivators for the ways we think, act, and interpret the world around us—something those with insecure attachment styles struggle with especially. The most common distortions that those with anxious attachment issues have to deal with are

- Catastrophizing. This distortion involves immediately jumping to the worst-case scenario. A partner being late getting home from work can turn irrationally into an elaborate story of them cheating, for instance.

- Emotional response. Emotional responses will be discussed more in just a moment.

- All-or-nothing thinking. An all-or-nothing mindset is one where everything is either one of two outcomes. Usually, it is as though if everything is not perfect, then the entire situation is the worst it could possibly be. For example, a "B" on a test can be perceived as a complete failure because it is not perfect.

- Personalizing. This distortion involves making everything about oneself, even if something occurred that was entirely unrelated to the person in question.

- Mind reading. As the name would suggest, mind reading involves believing that you already know how someone thinks or feels about a situation.

Of course, there are more cognitive distortions than that, but these are the ones that are most common to those who suffer from an anxious attachment style.

Emotional Responses and Anxious Attachment

A lot of people also suffer from emotional responses and reasoning as a result of their attachment style. Emotional reasoning often serves as a precursor to emotional response.

Emotional reasoning is a cognitive distortion that involves believing that because you feel some way, it must be an indicator of reality.

For instance, someone who suffers from anxious attachment might feel as though their relationship is falling apart. Then, because they *feel* this way, whether they have a reason or not, they begin to believe that their emotions are the way they are because their relationship truly is falling apart.

This is where emotional responses come into play. When someone with anxious attachment feels like this, and when they feel that their emotions are a direct indication of reality, then they start behaving in line with that. In line with our previous example, someone with anxious attachment and a tendency to respond emotionally might then treat their partner as though the relationship is falling apart. This, then, creates more distance and tension within the relationship.

The reason that this happens is because attachment styles have a strong influence on one's ability to regulate their emotions. This emotional regulation issue is one of the main obstacles to overcoming an anxious attachment style, but it can be trumped!

What Does Anxious Attachment Behavior Look Like?

In order to truly understand how and where anxious attachment behavior shows up in your relationships, take a look at the following examples of behavior:

- Your partner goes out and does not tell you where they are going or when they will be back. Instead of going about your day, you become fixated, crawling through social media to find clues, blowing up their phone, and worrying yourself half to death with anxiety.

- Your partner does not text you back right away, so when they see you next, you constantly ask for validation and assurance that they still love and care for you.

- Down to the punctuation in a text or a subtle shift in tone, you cannot help but overanalyze what your partner is saying—and usually, that analysis is negative.

- Because you fear that your partner will leave you for someone else, you begin to try and control who they speak to, where they go, and what they do, asserting yourself into their life at all costs.

All of these instances are points where anxious attachment leads to behavior that is not conducive to a healthy, happy relationship. This is why learning to break out of anxious attachment must be a priority in order to preserve and maintain strong relationships moving forward.

The Anxious Partner in Relationships

It is also important to delve into understanding the anxious partner dynamic more. Whether you are the anxious partner yourself, or if you are dating someone who has this attachment style, there are a lot of intricacies to be mindful of.

Dynamics of an Anxious Partnered Relationship

There are a lot of different dynamics that are at play when it comes to dating with an anxious attachment style somewhere in the mix. Some of those dynamics may include:

- Excessive worry. One common dynamic of an anxious partner in a relationship is worrying excessively about different parts of the relationship. This can include worrying about their partner's feelings, the future of the relationship, or even potential conflicts that may not even occur. Such worrying can lead to the constant need for reassurance.

- Fear of abandonment. A strong fear of abandonment or rejection by an anxious partner can cause them to cling to their partner or become possessive or jealous in an attempt to fend off that abandonment.

- Insecurity. Anxious partners are known to struggle with insecure feelings, specifically that they are not good enough to date their partner. Again, this can lead to seeking constant reassurance and validation from their partner.

- Jealousy and possessiveness. Anxious partners often feel jealousy when it comes to their partner. It is common that they imagine worst-case scenarios or feel threatened by friends and family of their partner, which can lead to controlling and possessive actions.

- Need for constant communication. Someone who is anxiously attached might find constant communication with their partner necessary. When apart, constant texts, calls, or messages may be the expectation—and the anxious partner becomes highly upset when that need cannot be met.

- Overanalyzing and overthinking. An anxious partner undoubtedly has a tendency to overanalyze situations and behaviors within their relationship. As a result, they read too far into minor details, which creates unneeded stress and conflict.

- Physical symptoms. Those who experience relationship anxiety also have to deal with physical symptoms. These can include, but are not limited to, restlessness, stomach aches and nausea, and heart palpitations. Anxiety can even make you feel sick, which can interfere with one's ability to engage in a healthy relationship.

- Trust issues. This is a highly common dynamic that those who are anxiously attached within relationships face. They might feel like they cannot trust the intentions of their partner, or that their partner is not loyal. And the tension is only furthered by the fact that these trust issues are usually present with no evidence of wrongdoing.

All of the above also have the ability to put a unique strain or tension onto a relationship. Each of these dynamics plays a unique role when it comes to influencing relationships, and by being mindful of these dynamics, you are one step closer to overcoming the pull of anxious attachment within your relationships.

Anxious Attachment Sabotage Strategies

In addition to the above dynamics, there are a few sabotage strategies that those with an anxious attachment style use and, therefore, break down their relationships thanks to. Even if unintentional, the sabotage strategies still have a significant impact.

For example, a lot of people who are anxiously attached have a tendency to be passive-aggressive, especially if something occurs that hurts them in some way. For example, if a partner returns home late from work, the next few hours might be littered with small jabs and passive-aggressive statements about that lateness, even slipping accusations into the mix.

This can make someone feel guilty even when they have no reason to. It is a poor communication tactic that sabotages many relationships, anxious or otherwise.

In addition, self-neglect can be observed in these relationships. If someone does not feel cared for or wants to force someone to care for them in a particular way, they might slip into the habit of neglecting their own needs. As a result, tension is placed on the other partner—they do not even know that they are meant to be doing something, and instead are forced to worry about their partner.

Anxiously attached individuals may also try to guilt trip or control their partner in order to find assurance within the relationship. This can mean making someone feel bad for hanging out with a friend, preventing them from spending time alone, or otherwise interfering with their ability to live an independent life with freedom.

Not all anxiously attached individuals do these things, and many do not even recognize that they are doing these things. This highlights the importance of proper communication and healing strategies in the face of an anxious attachment style.

You have explored the emotional rollercoaster that often accompanies this attachment pattern, gaining a deeper understanding of why you may experience the highs and lows of love in the way you do. You have taken the first step toward transforming anxiety into confidence and building more secure, lasting relationships. We now embark on a transformative path. Let's explore actionable strategies that will empower you to navigate love and connection with newfound confidence.

CHAPTER 3

Thriving in Anxious Attachment Love

Renew, release, let go. Yesterday's gone. There's nothing you can do to bring it back. You can't "should've" done something. You can only DO something. Renew yourself. Release that attachment. Today is a new day!
—Steve Maraboli

In the last chapter, we talked about the signs, influences, and dynamics that are involved when someone is in a relationship that involves an anxious attachment style. Knowing that information is half the battle; now, it's time to unveil how you can transform anxious behaviors, foster emotional security, and build relationships grounded in trust and mutual support. This chapter is your roadmap to achieving greater relationship confidence and lasting love.

Tips to Fix an Anxious Attachment Style (or Cope With Anxious Attachment Triggers)

You don't have to let anxious attachment be the leading characteristic of your relationship. It's time to take control of anxious attachment by using evidence-based strategies to fight it off. There are plenty of strategies, exercises, and techniques that can help you move from anxious to secure.

Simple Strategies for Anxious Attachment

There are dozens, if not hundreds, or even thousands, of strategies that you can use to overcome anxious attachment. This chapter focuses on a lot of those methods in detail, but let's get you started with some simple tips that will underscore your journey:

- Become aware of your attachment style. By now, you should have a strong idea of what your attachment style is; however, if you skipped the Attachment

Styles Quiz provided to you in Chapter 1, it is time to go back to that now. These strategies are not for avoidant attachment styles, so you may be putting in a lot of effort with no progress if you have wrongly identified your attachment style.

- Adjust your behavior. Adjusting your behavior is the crux of the solution. Most of your work has to be focused on replacing or improving behaviors that are toxic or due to your attachment style, which is something you will focus on throughout this chapter.

- Reach out to someone you trust. Ideally, you should find a friend or family member that you can reach out to, who *is not* your partner. Sometimes, an outside perspective can be exactly what we need to make change happen and get the insight we need to grow.

- Work on past issues. By now, it is clear that attachment issues form in childhood. This means that you have to really work on resolving those past issues and traumas that have led you to where you are today. It is hard work, but work that you must be dedicated to if you hope to move on from an anxious—or any insecure—attachment style.

- Define your needs and values. Everyone has needs and values. By taking the time to understand what is important to you, as well as what you *reasonably* expect from a relationship, you can work toward attaining the proper treatment in a relationship.

- Maintain open communication. As you work to improve your attachment style, there should always be open communication between yourself and your partner. Whether you like it or not, your partner has been impacted by your attachment style. A simple statement like "I'm sorry for how my actions have impacted you; I'm learning to manage my attachment issues better" can mean a lot to them.

- Focus on yourself. It is tempting and easy to focus on your partner as you work to overcome attachment issues. Instead, make the effort to focus on yourself and your growth. Not only will this help you heal, but you will actually notice that your relationships become stronger as a result.

- Date someone with a secure attachment. If you are not dating right now, making sure that you date people with secure attachment styles can be a good step forward. A lot of the time, dating others with attachment issues can only reinforce our unhealthy attachment habits.

- Slowly practice detachment. Work on developing detachment from your relationships, and instead of defining yourself through your relationships, work on developing independence.

- Know that protest behavior won't work. Acting out or acting harshly toward your partner to get them to behave how you want is not going to improve your relationship; it will only damage it more.

- Amp up your self-care. Caring for yourself shows that you are worthy and boosts confidence, which can counteract signs of anxious attachment.

Remember that Rome was not built in a day, much like progress is not achieved overnight. Not only do you have to work strongly at implementing these strategies, but you also have to make it a point to avoid unhelpful habits when symptoms are at an all-time high.

Unhelpful Habits to Avoid

At the same time as you work on yourself, you cannot expect things to go your way if you continue to engage in unhelpful habits—and there are many that you do engage with as a result of your attachment style. It is important to break out of those habits while reinforcing positive ones.

For example, a lot of individuals who are anxiously attached tend to make themselves too available. Rather than enjoying life independently and having fun on your own, you might have life set up so that you can answer messages as soon as they come in, or so that you can respond to anyone immediately. This both neglects your needs and furthers your attachment issues, which is why working to detach is so important.

In addition, a lot of people who deal with anxious attachment tend to have self-harm tendencies. Self-harm is not always what the movies or TV make it out to be. Harming yourself in any way, including by neglecting your needs or putting yourself into uncomfortable situations, is still self-harm. Rather than bending to self-harm desires, try to channel that energy into self-care instead.

Something else that a lot of people with an anxious attachment style cater to is savior fantasies. These are fantasies that involve believing that someone will swoop down and be perfect for you, fulfilling every need that you have in a manner that is unyielding. However, because you have unrealistic needs due to insecure attachment, that is not going to happen—and believing it will is a bad habit that damages current and future relationship prospects.

Finally, you should stop going out of your way to prove your worth to other people, and there are two reasons for this:

1. The right person will see your inherent worth as a human being without you having to prove anything. You do not—and should not—have to prove your worth to be treated properly by other people.

2. Going out of your way to prove your worth is a clear sign of attachment issues, which allows the wrong people to take advantage of that and use you, knowing that you are working on healing.

By breaking these bad habits of attachment, you and your partner will both benefit and have a stronger, healthier connection.

Affirmations for Anxiously Attached People

Affirmations are a wonderful way to amplify your healing. Your brain cannot tell the difference between reality and a strong visualization or affirmation. This means that you can use affirmations to help you overcome struggles caused by anxious attachment. Some affirmations that you can use include

1. I am deserving of love and security.
2. I trust in the strength of my emotional connections.
3. I am learning to soothe my own anxiety.
4. I can create healthy boundaries in my relationships.
5. I am open to receiving love and support.
6. I am not defined by my past attachment experiences.
7. I release the need for constant reassurance.
8. I embrace vulnerability as a source of strength.
9. I am capable of cultivating secure attachments.
10. I can communicate my needs and feelings effectively.

If you are looking for more affirmations, I have 40 more that you can download on my website—JoyceTbooks.com with Access Code **SECURE**— was well. Now that you have those affirmations, though, what are you meant to do with them? Do not worry—I have a few tips for you.

Tips for Your Affirmations Practice

First and foremost, it is good to use those affirmations as prompts. I strongly encourage you to create your own affirmations using those as a guide for your journey. A personalized affirmation works far better than prescribed ones because they target your specific goals and values. You can certainly use the above affirmations as they are, but you really amp up your practice by customizing them.

When you do use your affirmations, you should say them out loud and try to truly connect to the words that you are saying. You can idly say, "I am worthy of love," but the benefits only truly arise when you find some belief in those words. State them to yourself with conviction and confidence, even if it is at a low level—over time, you will become more confident in your affirmations.

Additionally, it is a good idea to spend 30 minutes a day reciting your affirmations. It takes 30 minutes a day for your brain to create neural pathways, which is why this is the perfect duration of time to practice your affirmations. In other words, your brain needs 30 minutes a day of consistent effort to believe or rewire itself. Your daily affirmation practice does just that.

Overall, it is important to remain consistent with your affirmations. Remember that you are not going to see results right away, but over time, if you are consistent and present as you recite your affirmations, you will notice big successes when it comes to your attachment mindset.

Mindfulness for Anxious Attachment

Another technique to help positively influence your attachment style is mindfulness. Mindfulness involves developing present awareness of what is going on in your mind and physically around you. It is a practice that intertwines with spirituality, psychology, and many other aspects of growth, and it can also help you break free from the shortcomings of your attachment style.

There are dozens of techniques that you can use to help you with anxious attachment. And mindfulness works because it pulls you out of your head and into the real world, where you can observe activities and ongoings through an objective or neutral lens. Two of my favorite (and the most effective) mindfulness activities for anxious attachment are box breathing and grounding.

Box Breathing

As I mentioned, box breathing is an effective tactic for helping with your anxious attachment style. So, what is box breathing? Box breathing is a breathing and relaxation technique where you take slow, deep breaths in a specific pattern. Usually, you are going to follow a pattern of inhale, hold, exhale, hold for equal lengths of time. Most commonly, the steps to box breathing are as follows:

1. Visualize a square in your mind. As you inhale for a count of four, trace up the left-hand side of the box.

2. Trace the top of the box as you hold your breath for the same four count.

3. Then, exhale. As you do so, trace down the right-hand side of the square.

4. Hold your breath for a final four count as you trace the bottom.

5. Repeat the process until you feel relaxed and at ease.

For some people, box breathing can feel like a very clinical practice; it does not have to be. You can feel free to customize box breathing and use the following tips to make the practice your own:

- Make sure that you are practicing box breathing in a comfortable position. You can technically box breathe anywhere and at any time, but if you are actually comfortable when you do so, you will be more likely to continue the practice.

- Relax your body as you do this activity. Breathing and relaxation are wonderful for alleviating tension, and if you relax your body while engaging in the breathing activity, you will find the practice to be more beneficial.

- Use visualization to amplify your practice. Box visualization is more than just a fun little thing to do—it is a visualization practice with known benefits when it comes to relaxation.

- Keep practicing and be consistent to actually benefit from the practice.

You might be wondering how exactly box breathing is supposed to benefit you when it comes to anxious attachment. There are a few ways in which this works. For instance, box breathing helps regulate the nervous system. This can reduce the body's fight or flight response that is associated with anxiety, helping you feel more grounded as a result.

In addition, box breathing helps with emotional regulation. Anxious attachment often results in emotional responses and a fear of abandonment, but box breathing can help you be more mindful and regulate these responses. As a result, you are more likely to communicate healthily and experience less impulsive behavior.

Grounding Techniques

Grounding techniques can also be used to help you feel less of the symptoms of anxious attachment. One of the most common grounding techniques is called the five senses grounding technique. Often taught in cognitive behavioral therapy (CBT), the five senses exercise goes like this:

- Start by naming five things that you can see. It can be anything from the scene around you to the fingerprints on your hands.

- Name four things that you can touch. Even if you have to get up to touch them, do so. Allow yourself to notice the texture of each item.

- Name three things you can hear. If you are in a quiet area, you can make small tapping, snapping, or popping sounds with your hands and notice those sounds.

- Name two things you can smell. Feel free to get up and light a candle, smell some lotion, or otherwise find a pleasant scent.

- Name one thing you can taste.

Make sure that you mindfully focus on each aspect of the practice individually and mindfully. Take in all of the aspects of each piece of sensory input and try to be present in the experience. This activity will calm you down and enhance your emotional regulation.

Positive Reframing: Challenge Your Negative Thoughts

Another tactic that you need to master in order to overcome the setbacks from anxious attachment is positive reframing.

Positive reframing involves taking negative thoughts, usually ones that are unhelpful or distorted, and turning them into positive or even neutral thoughts. These new thoughts are usually more reflective of reality, which can allow you to cope, heal, and grow with ease. Let's learn how you can reframe and challenge your negative thoughts.

Examples of Negative Thoughts

One of the most common statements that I hear from others is "I do not have negative thoughts," or even "My negative thoughts are not *that* bad!" Unfortunately, this stems from uncertainty surrounding negative thoughts—the fundamental misunderstanding of what a negative thought is. Some common examples of negative thoughts that individuals with anxious attachment have include

- I am unworthy of love and affection.
- I need constant reassurance to feel secure in my relationships.
- I am too needy and dependent on others.

- I am afraid of being abandoned or rejected by my partner.

- My partner is going to leave me, no matter what I do.

- I am not good enough for my partner.

- I have to constantly adapt myself to my partner's needs to maintain their love and attention.

- I am not capable of forming a healthy and stable relationship.

- I am always going to be let down by others.

- I am not lovable.

When you learn to recognize these negative thoughts, you gain the ability to overcome them. Generally, you can identify a negative thought by identifying a negative *feeling*, and then determining what you were thinking just before that feeling occurred.

Questions to Ask for Reframing

When you are tasked with the battle of reframing your negative thoughts, you might be wondering how you should begin to tackle such a mammoth task. The good news is that there are a few common questions and ideas you can begin with to get started:

- Is this thought true? A fact of life that you need to come to terms with is that not everything you think is necessarily true. Sometimes, doubts and anxieties can feel true without having any logic or reality to back them up.

- Is there any evidence that supports or contradicts this thought? Go through and write down—yes, on paper—the thoughts and evidence that support *and* contradict the thought.

- If this thought is true, what's the worst thing that could happen? Give yourself space to realistically consider what the worst thing that can happen is. Chances are, if you are being realistic, the worst is not often going to be *that* bad.

- What's the best-case scenario, and how likely is it to happen? Now, realistically consider the best-case scenario and its likelihood.

- Am I jumping to conclusions? Consider whether you are trying to predict the future or assume that something will happen without evidence.

- Am I overgeneralizing or catastrophizing? Think about whether you are trying to focus on the worst, or if you are making sweeping statements about a situation without considering its intricacies.

- Would I say this to a friend or loved one in the same situation? Sometimes, we are harsher to ourselves than necessary. If you cannot say the same thing you are thinking to a loved one, then you should not say it to yourself.

- Is this thought helping me or hurting me?

- Can I reframe this thought in a more positive or realistic way?

- How would I feel if I let go of this thought?

When you take into consideration questions like the ones above, you can start the process of reframing and uncovering whether or not your thought is actually realistic, helpful, and true.

A Simple, 3-Step Method

It might seem like reframing negative thoughts is complicated, but it is not! In fact, it can be broken down into three steps:

1. Identify your negative thinking. Your reframing begins with identifying negative thoughts. The best way to do so is to start with emotions—if you are feeling negative, then there was probably an underlying thought that created such a feeling. Consider what you were thinking before you felt that negative feeling and you will probably be able to isolate your negative thought.

2. Determine the thoughts to reframe. Now, try to isolate your negative thoughts, ideally by writing them down so that you can thoroughly understand what the thought or thoughts may be.

3. Reframe your thoughts. Finally, you have to work to reframe those negative thoughts!

Other Tips for Positive Reframing

Before sending you off to the next component of overcoming anxious attachment, I have some final tips for positively reframing your negative thoughts. For example, it is important to give yourself grace. If you are hard on yourself during this process, which is undoubtedly a challenge, you will not find yourself overcoming those negative thoughts. Instead, you should be kind to yourself so that you have the strength and resilience to grow and overcome those negative thoughts. Above all, prioritize patience and self-compassion.

In addition, it is important to use positive affirmations. Positive affirmations can help you reframe negative thoughts quickly and with confidence. By stating positive affirmations to yourself, you do not have to feel negatively influenced by thoughts because you are confidently creating neural networks that shift those thoughts.

Finally, be sure to surround yourself with positive people. When negative people are all around you, it feels impossible to break out of such a vacuum of negative thinking; however, when positive people are all around you, then it is easier to be kind and patient to yourself, understanding of your situations, and more.

Emotional Awareness and Regulation

The next way for you to work on tamping down your anxious attachment symptoms involves emotional awareness and regulation. Emotional awareness and regulation can be particularly challenging for those with anxious attachment issues because emotional awareness and regulation skills are often learned in childhood. And as a result of a caregiver disconnect in childhood, you might not have these skills already—but fret not, because you are about to learn them.

What Is Emotional Regulation?

Before we tackle how you can master emotional regulation, you have to start with a good framework of what emotional regulation is. Let's spend some time exploring what emotional regulation truly is.

Simply put, emotional regulation refers to your ability to manage and control your emotions. This includes all of the strategies that you have for identifying and modifying emotional responses to the world around you. There are several different core ideas that are involved in emotional regulation:

- Awareness. Emotional regulation begins with being aware of your emotions. You should be able to recognize and label your feelings, no matter what kind they are.

- Acceptance. It is also fundamental to accept that your varying emotions are a part of life, thus reducing self-judgment.

- Understanding triggers. Earlier, we talked about some of the emotional triggers faced by those with an anxious attachment style. Understanding and being able to identify those triggers is key to quality emotional regulation.

- Coping strategies. Anyone with strong powers of emotional regulation has healthy coping strategies under their belt—ones that help them relax, remain mindful, and otherwise regulate emotions.

We are going to work on each and every one of these strategies as we move forward. And beyond just being a useful tool for anyone, emotional regulation *and* emotional intelligence are particularly helpful for anxious attachment!

Emotional Intelligence and Anxious Attachment

Now that you are aware of what emotional regulation is and what it consists of, you are probably wondering how this can help with your specific anxious attachment struggles. When you have strong emotional regulation, you are likely emotionally *intelligent* as well! This is what helps you attach more securely—allow me to explain.

When you have anxious attachment issues, you feel a desire to be close to others and feel reassured; these emotions are in constant battle with abandonment and obsession in relationships. This is exactly what emotional intelligence can help mitigate. For example, emotional intelligence heightens your self-awareness. In turn, when you are more self-aware, you can recognize when you are triggered, as well as why you were triggered.

Additionally, emotional intelligence helps with self-regulation. When you understand your emotions, your capacity to regulate those emotions is enhanced. This, in turn, benefits your ability to develop the necessary skills for self-regulation that result in less conflict as a result of your attachment style.

Effective communication and social skills stem from emotional intelligence as well, both of which are immensely positive for someone who has an anxious attachment style. Emotional intelligence helps you communicate what you are feeling with others, which can help in allowing for your needs to be met. Furthermore, you can maintain secure attachments through skills like active listening, conflict resolution, cooperation, and more. Such social skills can make you more effective at navigating relationships.

In all, it is important to seek emotional regulation through emotional intelligence because it can emphasize strong and healthy connections within your life. Without emotionally intelligent behavior, you cannot overcome unhealthy attachment styles.

Skills and Strategies

Alright, so now you want to know how you can truly build up emotional regulation skills and become an emotionally intelligent boss in the face of anxious attachment. How can you do that? Well, the following skills are all you need to be emotionally intelligent and manage your symptoms:

- Accepting your emotions. Many people suffer from poor emotional regulation because they spend so much time trying to push their "negative" emotions away. Instead, accept your emotions, good or bad, as a part of you—and *not* a reflection of you! In doing so, you become more realistic with self-expectations, as well as more open to self-awareness.

- Identify and reduce triggers. Earlier, we talked about myriad emotional triggers that may be common for you. In order to be more emotionally intelligent, you not only have to identify those triggers but do what you can to healthily eliminate them as well.

- Practicing mindfulness. Mindfulness is all about accepting the present moment and whatever it has to offer. By practicing mindfulness, you harness the ability to understand what—and why—you are feeling in the moment, without delays or obstructions to understanding your emotions. This can help you identify triggers and overcome anxious attachment symptoms.

- Reappraisal. There is more than one side to every story, just like there is more than one side to every emotion. Before finding yourself certain that things are the way you think, consider whether things can be viewed from a different lens or perspective.

- Seeking emotional support. It is okay to reach out to others and be in need of support, and I even encourage it. As long as your emotions are not becoming dependent on the feelings or expectations of another person, then emotional support can be invaluable when it comes to validating and overcoming some of the more negative aspects of your attachment style.

- Self-awareness. One thing that is unavoidable when it comes to emotional regulation is self-awareness. There are many different methods that can help you attain self-awareness, including reflection, mindfulness, accepting yourself, and asking others for feedback.

- Self-compassion. How often has being negative to yourself actually granted you progress? Chances are, the answer is "rarely," if not "never." Give being compassionate toward yourself a chance, allowing yourself to truly accept that life is full of challenges and you are not perfect. It is okay to accept this, and it is good for your healing.

- Self-soothing. Something else that you can add to your toolkit for overcoming anxious attachment symptoms is self-soothing. Rather than looking to other people—like your partner, for example—to tackle the brunt of your emotional overwhelm, develop skills that empower you to handle your emotions instead.

- Tune in to physical symptoms. Your emotions are not always in your head; sometimes, the symptoms of anxious attachment can manifest physically. By being mindful of your physical symptoms as well, you can understand when you are feeling the pulls of anxious attachment more effectively.

Remember that practice makes perfect; over time, you will see the results of your work pay off if you remain consistent and positive.

Setting Healthy Boundaries

The last major tactic for thriving with anxious attachment is setting healthy boundaries. Setting healthy boundaries is instrumental to anyone experiencing a healthy relationship, but because those who are anxiously attached often struggle with boundaries, it can be even more important! Let's explore some of the reasons why healthy boundaries matter, as well as how you can set such boundaries.

Why Boundaries Matter

I cannot count the number of times that someone has told me, "Oh, my boundaries do not matter." Boundaries are more important than you know, and *everyone* has them. Think about something that you would, under no circumstances, want someone to treat you like. That's just one boundary that you have, whether you communicate it or not.

And communicating boundaries is vital. Essentially, boundaries are limitations that we put on other people regarding how they can and cannot treat us. Boundaries are not just something that we impose upon others to be cruel; rather, boundaries are crucial to being treated in a way that makes us feel safe, respected, and comfortable with others.

When you have an anxious attachment style, then it is likely that you never learned how to properly set boundaries. You might make yourself too available for others, or you may even violate the boundaries of others because you do not understand their importance.

Boundaries are what keep us from feeling bad when we spend time with others. And no matter how silly your boundary may seem, it is there for a reason—anyone who truly cares about you will respect your boundaries, and you should do the same for them.

How to Set Boundaries

After living a life with an insecure attachment style, setting boundaries might seem like an altogether foreign concept. How should you set and communicate your boundaries to other people in a way that is both respectful and assertive?

Start by visualizing and naming your boundaries. You cannot communicate your boundaries to someone else if they are not clear to you. Think about what your boundaries are and visualize them being respected, before putting them into a concise sentence that helps you understand your boundaries.

After that, you can communicate them to others. Let's say that you have a boundary where you do not like being hugged without someone asking first, and you have a friend who is a huge hugger. You can communicate your boundary assertively and respectfully by saying something like, "Hey, I appreciate that you show your affection so openly, but unannounced physical contact makes me super uncomfortable. I would feel better if you asked before hugging me next time!"

Saying something like that so openly and with vulnerability can definitely be scary; however, it is something you *have* to work on in order to be more respectful to yourself and work on those attachment struggles. It is also important that you actually commit to that boundary, and you do not let your friend hug you without permission once or then go back and forth with you when you enforce it. This allows people to believe that they can disregard your boundaries.

Of course, you do not have to set every boundary in the world right away. You can start off small by setting just a few boundaries with people whom you trust before moving into setting more ambitious or frightening boundaries.

One of the scariest things can be setting boundaries for yourself when you have never done so before. But over time, it becomes much easier to both set and enforce your boundaries to others, ensuring that you are receiving appropriate treatment from everyone.

Handling Those Who Disrespect Your Boundaries

The unfortunate news out of all of this is that not everyone will respect your boundaries. It is so easy for those with anxious attachment styles to become involved with people who do not have their best interests in mind. That's why you have to know the following steps to handling boundary disrespect:

1. Remind them of your boundaries. If someone crosses a boundary, kindly remind them of your boundary. You do not have to explain *why* you have a particular boundary (unless you want to disclose that).

2. If they continue to violate your boundary, even "accidentally," then it is time to bring in a consequence. Let them know that if they cannot respect you and your boundaries, then you will have to distance yourself from them for your safety and comfort.

3. Follow through. If they keep behaving in a way that disrespects your boundaries, then it is time to cut them off.

Remember that setting boundaries might be hard at first, but over time, you will come to appreciate all that they do for you—including the amplified self-respect that you have and the ease with which secure attachment comes to you.

Relationship Strengthening Activities

Anxious attachment is often the result of feeling disconnected or distant from your partner.9This can be resolved by taking the time to work on strengthening your relationship in healthy ways, as opposed to forming more unhealthy attachment bonds like jealousy and clinginess. Furthermore, healthy attachment can even help dissolve unhealthy or insecure attachment tendencies.

There are hundreds of ways that you can work to strengthen your relationship, including

- Eye contact. Making eye contact is one of the fastest ways to bond and experience trust between yourself and another person. Make sure to make eye contact with one another in conversation.

- Hair care. You and your partner can engage in hair care together as a way to bond! For instance, you can take turns washing each other's hair—an intimate act that can bond you. Brushing or styling one another's hair is a good option as well.

- Touch. Touch and skin-to-skin contact are among the most valuable ways that human beings bond. It is how attachment forms and is solidified in a healthy way. You and your partner can bond through touch by massaging lotion into each other's hands, hugging or cuddling, or even playing hand games like thumb wars!

- Vulnerability. Naturally, vulnerability will help you and your partner connect on a stronger level. You can work on vulnerability by expressing your emotions, being open about insecurities, and sharing your aspirations.

In order to work with these methods, I recommend picking one or two that you want to start with and practicing those methods with your partner. Then, as you feel more comfortable, expand into other ways of connecting!

Remember that change is possible. By implementing the strategies outlined in this chapter, you are taking significant steps toward breaking free from the grip of anxiety and building relationships grounded in confidence and fulfilled in love. The next chapter explores the fascinating realm of avoidant attachment styles.

CHAPTER 4

When Love Feels Elusive

You can have anything you want if you are willing to give up the belief that you cannot have it.
–Dr. Robert Anthony

If you have ever felt the urge to maintain emotional independence in your relationships or found it challenging to fully open up to love, you might discover elements of avoidant attachment within yourself. In this chapter, we will delve into the nuances of avoidant attachment. Trust me, you'll walk out of here with a complete understanding of where avoidant attachment style comes from and what it looks like in your life.

Avoidant Attachment 101

As with anxious attachment, we are going to cover the intricacies of how to overcome avoidant attachment in detail. But in order to do that, we first have to have a strong springboard and foundation regarding what exactly the avoidant attachment style is!

Signs of Avoidant Attachment

Understanding what avoidant attachment looks like is best done by taking a look at the signs. After all, the signs of avoidant attachment style are fairly different from the signs one experiences when they have an anxious attachment style, so you should find the ability to differentiate between the two fairly easily.

One of the biggest indicators of avoidant attachment is trouble with handling conflict. Someone who is avoidant will, rather than getting involved or even trying to soothe the conflict, remove themselves from the situation entirely. And this goes beyond merely taking a second to compose themselves; someone with this attachment style tends to try and avoid conflict at all costs, never viewing conflict as the potentially positive influence it can be.

In addition, those with an avoidant attachment style have trouble reading emotions. Due to rather inconsistent caregivers giving them an unrealistic idea of what a range of emotions should look like, it can be hard for someone with this attachment style to tell if others are angry, sad, or even happy. This makes it even harder to be trusting, communicative, and otherwise exist within harmonious relationships with others.

In fact, being unable to be emotionally available and vulnerable is one of the hallmarks of avoidant attachment. Childhood experiences lead to the expectation that one has to bottle up or suppress their emotions, thus making it difficult for someone with avoidant attachment symptoms to actually connect to those around them in a meaningful and vulnerable way.

Moreover, someone who has an avoidant attachment style is unlikely to put themselves into a situation where they have to be reliant upon others. Due to unreliable caregivers, relying on others in adulthood is like an uphill battle; the avoidant-attached individual feels as though everyone will respond with the same lack of consistency to their needs.

If you suffer from avoidant attachment, then it is also likely that you strive to suppress negative emotions or emotional needs that you have. This also stems from childhood, from a place of not having your emotional needs met or even having them responded to in an abusive way. Therefore, it becomes second nature to hide negative emotions or emotional needs to avoid eliciting the same response from others—including your own partner.

Feeling repulsed by intimacy is not uncommon either. Intimacy is an uncommon feeling, and such closeness and vulnerability can feel, quite frankly, gross to some individuals with an avoidant attachment style. Naturally, feeling this way makes it hard, if not impossible, to form close relationships with other people.

Those who deal with avoidant attachment strive for independence above all else. Relying on someone for something, no matter how trivial it may seem, can be one of the worst situations for someone with avoidant attachment style to be in. In fact, they are attracted to unavailable individuals, because those people are characteristically unreliable and will not be dependable at all.

If you recognize yourself in any of these signs, then you might just have an avoidant attachment style. Now, we have to unveil what brings up those emotions—because they often have to be triggered to show up!

Avoidant Attachment Triggers

As with anxious attachment, triggers are the primary reason why attachment issues come into play. Existing alone and on a normal day will not just entice you to have attachment issues; they usually peak as a result of a trigger of some sort. The most common triggers for those with avoidant attachment are

- Someone expecting you to open up. People with avoidant attachment styles are very resistant to emotional vulnerability. As a result, being expected to open up can be jarring and trigger further avoidant behaviors, all in the name of avoiding potential hurt.

- Someone texts or calls them often. Such behavior may be perceived as clingy or expecting too much of someone with an avoidant attachment style. As a result, texts and calls in excess can cause someone to distance themselves and push others away.

- A partner wanting to get too close. If one's partner wants to form enhanced closeness or intimacy, someone with avoidant attachment issues might push them away or close themselves off emotionally to that person.

- Emotional intimacy and vulnerability. In fact, any level of emotional intimacy or vulnerability can trigger feelings of avoidance within someone who suffers from this attachment style and its associated symptoms.

- Receiving praises. Even something as simple as a "good job" or "thank you" from a partner can cause someone who is avoidant to shut down. The reason for this is that when one receives praise yet has this attachment style, praise becomes an expectation one always feels that they have to meet.

- Being criticized by respected friends and loved ones. Being criticized by respected individuals can be a knife in the heart to someone with an avoidant attachment style. This is because someone with this attachment style takes feeling criticized to be a failure.

- Their partner being too demanding. For someone who is avoidant, having too much demanded of them can make them shut down or feel the need to distance themselves even further from their partner. It feels like they are being set up for expectations that they are uncomfortable fulfilling.

- Feeling like the relationship is taking up too much of their time. Those with avoidant attachment style are almost the polar opposite of those who are anxiously attached; therefore, someone with avoidant attachment style is going to want to avoid spending too much time together as it makes them feel overwhelming intimacy that they are not comfortable with.

- It feels like someone is demanding their attention. Likewise, demands for attention can feel like forced intimacy, making someone who attaches avoidantly uncomfortable and distant.

- Their partner makes plans for future commitments. Such commitments can feel very restrictive for someone who attaches in this way; they feel as though they have to follow through with said commitments or else.

- Romantic gestures. Romantic gestures represent a form of intimacy that some people with avoidant attachment style are just not comfortable with. These displays of intimacy can make it hard for avoidant people to feel secure in relationships.

- A friend or partner is emotional and wants comfort. Even if someone is not dating a person with avoidant attachment issues, it can become hard for an avoidant person to offer comfort. Comfort is something that they did not receive much of as a child, so it is a very foreign concept.

- Physical contact and intimacy when they are not in the mood. Especially if they are not in the mood, physical contact can be a big trigger for avoidant tendencies.

And, of course, you may experience some (but not all) or even different triggers when your avoidant attachment style is called into question. Keep in mind that your experience does not have to match my words perfectly for it to be perfectly valid.

Unhealthy Habits of Avoidant People

As you can see, there are quite a few reasons behind what provokes someone to attach avoidantly, as well as what allows the main signs of that attachment style to show up. It is also important to be mindful of unhealthy habits that can arise from someone who is avoidant. Much like with anxious attachment style, there are a few different negative habits to be aware of.

One unhealthy habit of avoidant people involves focusing too much on factors of life that they can control. For example, someone with an avoidant attachment style might put their all into work. They may spend far too much time working and focusing on work-related affairs because this empowers them with a sense of control that they do not have in other areas of life. In the context of a relationship, this might look like someone being a workaholic or sacrificing bonding and time together for non-urgent work matters.

Another habit to be mindful of is the use of repression. When someone is avoidantly attached, this usually stems from cold and inconsistent caregivers in childhood. As a result of such treatment, emotions had to be managed through suppression so that they did not become a conflict of interest with an unkind caregiver. Unfortunately, this can rub off on adult life and result in relationships where, rather than discussing conflict and uncomfortable emotions, someone suppresses what they feel. This prevents problems from being resolved and can even create further problems.

In addition, someone with avoidant attachment style is likely to avoid asking for help and support from their loved ones, even when they need it. Inconsistent care in childhood is the reason for this as well; as a result, those with this style of attachment may go without much-needed care and assistance. It can also put a strain on their relationships since those around them will feel unworthy of being relied upon.

Sulking and complaining is also a common yet unhealthy habit for someone with an avoidant attachment style. Rather than asking for help directly, someone who is avoidant will take to complaining, sulking, or even breaking down rather than asking for help. If others step in, they may act as though they do not need help, or they may become angrier if others do not just know to step in and help.

Finally, those with an avoidant attachment style might engage with pre-emptive strategies to cope with their feelings. In other words, someone with an avoidant attachment style might feel that their relationship is collapsing and preemptively break up with their partner in order to engage in damage control.

In all, these unhealthy habits are unhealthy because they further the cycle of unhealthy attachment while also contributing to the damage of relationships around someone. Someone who deals with an avoidant attachment style is going to constantly feel uncomfortable and worried in a relationship, and these unhealthy habits are ways of managing their uncomfortable feelings.

With this knowledge of avoidant attachment, you can successfully identify avoidant attachment. However, you should also know what avoidant attachment can look like in action within a relationship, so let's transition and look at avoidant attachment in that context now.

The Avoidant Partner in Relationships

In any relationship, health and happiness cannot be assured if someone has an avoidant attachment style. There are a lot of pitfalls, dynamic interplays, and more that contribute to how an avoidant attachment style can harm a relationship.

In a relationship where one or both partners have an avoidant attachment style, emotional distance is very present. Those who are avoidant in their attachment will often distance themselves as a protective measure, which results in a lack of intimacy and closeness with their partner. When one partner has a secure attachment style, and the other is avoidant, this can make the secure partner feel unwanted or unloved in the relationship. When someone with an anxious attachment style dates an avoidant person, it leads to a push-pull cycle that harms everyone involved.

Someone with an avoidant attachment style will have an immensely hard time expressing their emotions, even to their partner. In a healthy relationship, emotional communication and reliance on one's partner are good and normal; however, avoidant individuals cannot or will not express how they feel to their partner. This can cause conflicts to become bottled up, as well as decrease intimacy, making the other partner feel detached from the relationship.

For someone with an avoidant attachment style, the desire for independence is strong. Many people who are in a relationship with someone who is avoidant state that it feels like they are not even in a relationship because the avoidant individual is so independent and lacks connection with the fundamentals of the relationship.

Typical Relationship Dynamics

Within a relationship with an avoidant individual, there are a few dynamics that are usually—if not always—at play during the relationship. Some dynamics you may notice include:

- Independence-intimacy cycle. As I mentioned, those with an avoidant attachment style often crave independence. They do not want to rely upon anyone for anything, but at times, that independent drive can abate. People with an avoidant attachment style are capable of being intimate, and often will be; however, that soon leaves and is replaced by independence once again. This hot-and-cold behavior can pose significant relationship issues.

- Mixed signals. The last point leads into the mixed signal dynamic that is often perpetuated within relationships. Someone constantly shifting between unyielding independence only to crave intimacy later sends mixed signals to a partner. This can reinforce a similar dynamic to the one from childhood, with inconsistency at its core.

- Fear of commitment. Another dynamic within a relationship with someone who is avoidant is a fear of commitment. Many people with an avoidant attachment style will be afraid of committing to a relationship because it makes them feel as though they are losing their independence. Long-term relationships can often be complicated because of this.

And while these dynamics are normal for a relationship with an avoidant person, they are not *healthy* dynamics by any means. Such dynamics contribute to distance, difficulty, and conflict within a relationship, often even resulting in the collapse of the relationship entirely.

Challenges in a Relationship With an Avoidant Partner

Dating an avoidant partner poses unique challenges to the relationship as well. For example, someone who is dating an avoidant partner may misinterpret the intentions of the avoidant partner. An avoidant partner may crave independence and, therefore, distance themselves from their partner. To them, they have not done anything wrong; they needed space, and they took it. But to their partner, it can feel as though the avoidant partner is not interested or does not care about their relationship.

This is only a further solidified issue because those who attach avoidantly struggle to communicate. To them, their distance seems obvious. Therefore, when a partner complains of feeling distant or left out, the avoidant partner is not sure of what to say or how to express their feelings—because emotional expression is, as mentioned, quite a challenge.

In addition, avoidant partners can create quite an emotional rollercoaster within a relationship. Going back and forth between intimacy and detachment, for instance, can create an emotional push and pull for both partners; a healthy partner will wonder why they are being treated so indifferently, and an avoidant partner will wonder why the healthy partner is responding in such a way.

Coupled with communication issues, many relationships between avoidant individuals can feel doomed. An avoidant partner will not be able to communicate their needs effectively, and at the same time, they will not be able to meet the emotional cues of their partner without conflict. Both partners can feel misunderstood, under-appreciated, and otherwise in a bad spot within the relationship.

What Can Be Done?

In the next chapter, we will explore the potential solutions in detail. However, it is good to take a look at some of the potential solutions ahead of time. Plus, other solutions than the ones covered in Chapter 5 may be helpful.

For example, it is okay to seek professional support if you need it, especially if you hope to preserve an existing relationship. If the individual who has an avoidant attachment style seeks help, for example, it can significantly have a positive impact on the trajectory of the relationship. Even couples counseling can be of benefit, helping everyone involved cope with clashing attachment styles without conflict.

It is also wise for the nonavoidant partner to seek solace in self-care. Remembering that someone's attachment style is not your fault is always wise. Rather than letting your partner's attachment style get you down, or even taking your frustrations out on them, it is a good idea to do two things. First, educate yourself on attachment styles. You are doing so right now, but really delving into why attachment styles exist and how they present can help you feel less isolated and frustrated. Second, make sure to take time to reflect on your personal boundaries and try to communicate them with your partner effectively. Your partner is not a mind reader, and oftentimes, communicating boundaries clears things up fast.

Beyond that, it is good for everyone in the relationship to make it a point to prioritize personal growth. If two people in a relationship are not both looking to attain personal growth, then one person will inevitably fall behind, failing to have their needs met or their desires satisfied. Self-reflection is, in this case, an invaluable tool for helping you and your partner get to know each other and yourself better.

Finally, I recommend finding a way to allow the avoidant partner to have an outlet for independence. Not everything has to be shared between a couple, and by fostering independence within a relationship, it becomes easier for someone with an avoidant attachment style to feel secure within the relationship.

You have uncovered the intricacies of avoidant attachment and recognized how it shapes your approach to love and intimacy. The next chapter explores strategies for moving from avoidant tendencies to secure connections, ultimately helping you create the lasting, fulfilling relationships you desire.

CHAPTER 5

Nurturing Love With Avoidant Healing

Cut the cords of attachment. Expand the circle of love.
–Shri Radhe Maa

So, you have identified that you are an avoidant person, and now you are familiar with the impact that this has on your life. That is an amazing first step into overcoming the challenges of this particular attachment style! Now, however, you need some tools to get you going with truly overcoming those obstacles.

In this chapter, you will gain access to a comprehensive set of exercises and strategies designed to address avoidant attachment patterns and nurture healthier, more secure bonds in romantic relationships. You will understand how to embrace vulnerability, increase emotional intimacy, and overcome the challenges associated with avoidant tendencies. It's a phenomenal way to break free from the shackles of your attachment style in order to love and be loved freely. Let's get started.

Benefits of Healing Avoidant Attachment

Before we get started with tools and strategies, it is a good idea to take a look at some of the ways that healing your attachment style can benefit you and your relationships moving forward. Not only will this give you something to look forward to on your journey, but it will help you continue to move forward when the road is bumpy.

First, healing an avoidant attachment style is known to increase self-awareness. Self-awareness is the skill wherein you know what you are feeling and why you are feeling it. Oftentimes, unhealthy attachment issues can make it difficult to understand why you feel or behave a certain way; on the other hand, when you have a healthy attachment style, you understand where your attachment concerns come from, what drives them, and how you can heal from them—ultimately heightening your self-awareness in the best way possible.

In addition, healing avoidant attachment also enhances the quality of your relationships. This might sound obvious, but when you are less avoidant in the face of love and intimacy, you can form stronger relationships with others that are meaningful to both parties. Less fighting will occur, the needs of everyone involved will be met, and relationships will head toward more pleasant futures rather than remaining stagnant. If you are someone with an avoidant attachment style in a relationship with a healthily attached person, the best gift that you can give to them and to your relationship is healing that attachment style.

Another benefit that you will receive as you work to heal an avoidant attachment style is enhanced emotional well-being. From the lens of having an avoidant attachment style, you might think that your emotional well-being is fine; however, those who attach with avoidance often lack the invaluable connection and support that *everyone* needs in order to maintain strong well-being—no matter the person. When you have a healthy attachment style, you can connect to others, receive support, and worry less about the ins and outs of a relationship that can otherwise be a challenge for those with unhealthy attachment styles.

Stronger self-worth accompanies healing avoidant attachment as well. For many people with an avoidant attachment style, it is hard to find worth in oneself. Criticism is taken harshly, but praise is, too, meaning that someone with this attachment style never understands their true self-worth. But when you work to develop a healthy attachment style, it becomes abundantly clear that your self-worth comes from within—and *not* from your relationships with others.

Better emotional regulation is another benefit you can expect from healing your attachment issues. Someone with an unhealthy style of attachment, no matter what that style may be, can struggle to control their emotions, often wavering between two extremes. Not only is this bad for their own well-being, but it is bad for any relationships they maintain, too. By healing your attachment style, you can regulate those emotions far better.

And finally, healing your attachment style is known to improve communication. As mentioned in Chapter 4, avoidant people cannot clearly communicate their needs, nor are they able to function responsibly in a conflict. However, when someone has a healthy attachment style, the needs of both partners can be communicated and problems can be resolved peacefully.

As you can see, there are so many benefits that accompany truly taking the time to heal an avoidant attachment style. And the good news? Every single one of those benefits is available to you. All you have to do is keep reading to find out how you can attain each and every one of those benefits, *and* apply them to your life and relationships moving forward.

Tips for Healing the Avoidant Attachment Style

Now, you understand why healing your attachment style is so important. Practically every area of your social and emotional life can be improved when you take the time to make healing a focal point of your life. But what can you do to actually begin the healing process?

Healing your attachment style is going to be a long process, which makes sense—it formed over the course of a long period of time, after all. Not everyone benefits from the same strategies and tools, so make sure to keep an open mind and explore. Some of the strategies that you can try include

- Take a journey back in time. Something that can be especially helpful is to try and determine where your attachment issues began. It can be hard to isolate the exact incident that led to your current style of attachment, but reflecting upon some of the scenarios in your childhood that made you feel unsupported or uncared for can help you better understand your triggers moving forward.

- Identify deactivating strategies. Deactivating strategies are used by avoidant individuals in order to deny their need for connection and remain self-reliant. We will dive into what deactivating strategies do and might look like in the next section.

- Recognize negative thinking and challenge it. Negative thinking is one of the easiest ways to remain trapped within an unhealthy cycle of thinking, and that includes your attachment style. Negative thoughts like "If I mess up, no one will love me" or "I do not need friends to be happy" can sabotage your relationships and overall happiness. Instead, challenging those negative thoughts rather than falling into them can allow you to have a more realistic outlook on your life, interactions, and the world around you.

- Practice expressing your feelings/connect to your emotions. Emotional expression and connection are, as you know by now, rather challenging for individuals who deal with an avoidant attachment style. Instead of clamming up when it comes to emotional expression, try talking to others and using statements like "I feel" or "I need." This will get you into the habit of expressing your emotions to other people.

- Go outside your comfort zone. You cannot heal from avoidant attachment—an attachment style that inherently involves being closed off—by lingering in your comfort zone. Therefore, it is going to be necessary to try new things and even make yourself a little uncomfortable in order to truly find yourself in a state of healing.

- Learn more about other people. You might not think that learning about other people could invite healing into your life, but it can! A lot of people who attach with an avoidant style have this idea that other people are going to behave similarly to how their caregiver(s) did. For example, if someone was unreliable in their care for you, you might think that *everyone* is going to be an unreliable figure—that is not the case. By learning more about other people, you do not have to wonder whether someone is going to be consistent. You will know based on their character.

- Make a relationship gratitude list. Independence is something everyone craves, but when you are feeling like isolating yourself, something that can help you get in touch with those around you and truly appreciate your relationships is a relationship gratitude list. Write down the facets of relationships and particular relationships, for which you are grateful. When you feel pangs of independence coming back in, you can revisit and add to the list.

- Get the support of a therapist. Sometimes, it is necessary to seek professional help like that of a therapist. Therapists are licensed and specialize in different areas, and there are, in fact, therapists who can help you with an avoidant attachment style. Through therapy, you can learn tools and strategies that you might not have been familiar with—even ones that this book cannot provide to you. Therapy might be a good option if you are someone who struggles with self-paced healing or needs more accountable options.

Healing is not a one-size-fits-all experience, which means that you are going to have to find what works for you. The good news is that the solutions do not end there; over the remaining duration of this chapter, you will be introduced to countless strategies and methods to supplement these foundational tips.

On Deactivating Strategies

Earlier, I mentioned something called deactivating strategies. Deactivating strategies are a common tactic used by individuals with avoidant attachment styles so that they can continue to avoid interpersonal relationships and connections. These harmful strategies serve as alternatives to real human connection, convincing someone who engages with them that it is not necessary to bond. Let's take a look at some of the common deactivating strategies that people with avoidant attachment issues use.

One deactivation strategy that is often used is physical distance. Someone with an avoidant attachment style might try to avoid physical contact and intimacy in order to keep their partner at bay, furthering their attachment issues and "independence." This might look like simple no's when asked for intimate interaction, or it might look like consistent excuses as to why intimacy is not alright at the moment. This is different from consent—someone using this deactivation strategy is doing so to avoid contact due to trauma, not a lack of desire.

Another deactivating strategy that is often used involves doubting one's feelings. Someone with an avoidant attachment style might crave intimacy or contact, only to then berate themselves and question whether they truly "need" that connection. They will doubt whether they truly like someone, wondering if it is just a temporary thing or something they made up in their head, and will doubt if they actually want to be with someone physically or emotionally. This extends beyond simply being unsure of themselves and instead involves constant rumination.

In addition, reflecting on a fear of not being enough can also serve as a deactivation strategy for someone with an avoidant attachment style. Commonly, avoidant individuals worry whether they are enough for a particular person, or even if they are enough for anyone. As a result, they might determine that no, they are not good enough, and, therefore, try to avoid contact and connection at all costs.

Overanalysis can be used as a deactivation strategy as well. When someone with an avoidant attachment style is in a relationship, they may overanalyze every little aspect of their relationship. Then, when they see a potential "failing" or mess up within the relationship, they use that as a potential way to break the relationship off or get out of the vulnerable position that they are in. They may overanalyze the situation before it even begins as well, giving themselves a reason to never enter into romantic endeavors.

Something else that a lot of individuals with avoidant attachment issues do is use fictional infatuation as a buffer. Whether consciously or not, it becomes easy to view fictional characters as ideal partners—not only because they are "perfect," but because intimacy cannot exist. Someone may "date" a fictional character in their head or spend so much time obsessing over a fictional character through media that they never have time to enter into any meaningful, real-life relationships. Our minds can, at times, struggle to tell reality from a vivid delusion, which makes this such a compelling deactivation strategy for many people with this attachment style.

Finally, someone might use past relationships as a deactivation strategy. This can work in two ways:

1. Someone was unreliable, unkind, or otherwise negative in a relationship. If a past relationship with a caregiver, partner, or friend was negative and fed into attachment issues, then someone who is avoidant may use this as an opportunity to avoid all future relationships. In their mind, the hurt that they suffered is inevitably going to happen again.

2. Someone was reliable, kind, or otherwise positive in a relationship. In the instance that someone breaks through the shell of avoidance, a positive past relationship can become a framework against which every new relationship is compared. "Nothing will be the same as [person]" is a common deactivating statement used by people with this attachment style.

As a result, rather than treating individuals as individuals, someone who uses this method may create sweeping generalizations that harm their relationships moving forward.

Not everyone with an avoidant attachment style is prone to engaging with deactivating strategies, but it is definitely something that a significant number of people with this attachment style are used to. Part of healing from avoidant attachment is overcoming these deactivating strategies and focusing on real, interpersonal relationships that you can only get with dedication and healing.

Avoidant Healing Strategy 1: Meditation

Now, it is time to really dig into methods that can help you heal, transforming your attachment style from avoidant to secure. The first healing strategy that I want to share with you is meditation. Believe it or not, meditation is more than just sitting down with your eyes closed—it is a powerful method that can help you transform your attachment style.

How Can Meditation Help?

Many people are in disbelief when I tell them that meditation can help cure their attachment style. There are five main ways in which you can heal your attachment style using meditation as a catalyst:

1. Increased self-awareness. Due to the reflection encouraged by meditation, you can find yourself being more aware of your thoughts, emotions, and behaviors. This can be particularly beneficial when it comes to recognizing avoidance patterns and determining why they exist.

2. Enhanced emotional regulation. People who are avoidant often have issues with expressing intimacy, and even go as far as suppressing their emotions. But because a core tenet of meditation involves judgment-free observation of emotions, meditation can help!

3. Stress reduction. Meditation is known to reduce stress. At the same time, chronic stress can make avoidance worse, which makes it hard to participate in close relationships. Because of this, meditation can help reduce stress and, therefore, empower you to attach more healthily.

4. Improved focus and concentration. Meditation has the power to improve your ability to focus and concentrate. What does this have to do with avoidant attachment? Well, some people with an avoidant attachment style struggle to remain present in social settings, instead zoning out and losing touch. When you meditate, this is not a concern.

5. Cultivating compassion and empathy. Certain types of meditation can actually help you be more empathetic to others, which is excellent for someone who is especially avoidant.

Even if you have never meditated before, breaking into the act of it and making meditation a habit is not hard. To get you started, we'll look at one of the most common methods of meditation: mindfulness meditation.

Mindfulness Meditation

Mindfulness meditation is one of the most common *and* effective forms of meditation. It is certainly helpful when it comes to achieving benefits associated with meditation for avoidance. Here are the steps to mindfulness meditation geared toward your particular attachment style:

1. Start by choosing a quiet and comfortable space where you will not be disturbed for a few minutes. Sit or lie down, or even feel free to pace back and forth if that is more comfortable for you. Maintain good posture, but try to avoid tensing up.

2. Set a time limit for your meditation. It's good to start with five or ten minutes, and then increase the time limit as you become more comfortable. Remember that consistency is more important than duration when it comes to meditation.

3. Bring your focus to your breathing. You should allow your eyes to close or gaze softly as you do. Take time to notice the sensation of each inhale and exhale, feeling the rise and fall of your body as you breathe. Do not force your breathing to follow any pace—just breathe naturally.

4. Now, allow yourself to be present. As you breathe, your mind may begin to wander. It's normal for that to happen, so do not berate yourself for your mind doing so. Just observe the presence of those thoughts, and then bring your attention back to your breathing. Spend a few minutes in this state before moving on to the next step.

5. Next, it is time for a body scan. You can perform a body scan by starting at your toes and moving up to

your head, observing each part of the body as you do. Pay attention to temperature, tension, pain, or any other sensation in each part of your body.

6. As you meditate, if any negative thoughts arise, acknowledge them. Even if you have to say "I acknowledge you" to the thought, just let that acknowledgement exist and then return your focus to the present.

Most people say that it takes up to three weeks to feel the benefits of meditation, so if something is not "working" right away, try giving it a bit more time. Meditation does not work overnight, so be patient and keep an open mind as you engage with it.

Visualization

The next strategy that you can use to work on your attachment style is visualization. Visualization is in the same category as meditation because visualization involves meditative focus to bring about a desired outcome. When you visualize, you imagine yourself as already having something or being in a position you desire.

Visualization is especially powerful when it comes to helping you overcome your avoidant attachment style. When you visualize something, your brain perceives it as if it were reality—so long as the visualization is strong and dedicated. With that being said, when you envision yourself in a healthy attachment situation, your mind allows you to heal and move closer to a healthy attachment style.

What's more, is that visualization is not a complicated process. In order to visualize something, you just have to

1. Decide what you are going to visualize. In order for your visualization to have an effect, you have to decide on what you are going to visualize. Maybe it is a healthy relationship dynamic for your current relationship, or maybe it is a partner who helps you grow. Pick something meaningful for you to visualize.

2. Calm your body and mind. You can do this by taking time to visualize, breathe deeply, or otherwise spend time soothing yourself.

3. Visualize what you selected. Imagine what it is that you want to visualize, and try to incorporate all five senses into the visualization if possible. This makes the visualization more realistic and easier to stick to.

And that's it! Visualization is not a complicated process, but it is one that definitely makes an impact when you take the time to engage with it. You can visualize as a solitary practice or couple it with meditation for enhanced benefits!

Avoidant Healing Strategy 2: Journaling

Another avoidant attachment healing strategy that I have for you is journaling. There are a lot of skeptics out there when it comes to the powers of journaling but think about it: The method would not be so popular if it did not work. With that being said, journaling can be an invaluable tool for self-reflection, harnessing emotional wisdom, and preventing you from acting on impulses that are not good for you. Let's take a look at how you can get into the habit of journaling for success.

Why Should I Journal?

There are so many good reasons for you to journal as a part of your process of healing. For example, journaling helps you recognize your patterns. Most people with avoidant attachment issues have a pattern that involves a trigger, an action, and then an outcome. When you take the time to journal—especially about particular events that pertain to your attachment—you can take note of these patterns and work to break them. This prevents needless cycles from occurring and impacting your ability to form relationships.

In addition, journaling is a wonderful tool for helping you process your emotions. When you feel rejected, imposed upon, or otherwise emotional when it comes to your attachment style, your first instinct may be to react. However, if you take the time to journal about those events and your feelings instead, you can process your emotions more intelligently and, therefore, react in a smarter, more appropriate manner.

Journaling is also a process that allows you to discover yourself more meaningfully. As you journal, not only do you gain the ability to work through problems, but you also come to learn more about yourself. Journaling is one of the fastest ways that you can become your own best friend, learning about your dreams, motivations, likes and dislikes, and more.

This is a practice that is far more than just jotting some words down on paper aimlessly—journaling is a psychologically approved manner of processing emotions, working through problems, growing, and otherwise finding benefit in our lives. Now that you understand why journaling can be so useful, it is time to look at how you can attain such benefits!

Journaling Tips

Telling someone to journal is not very self-explanatory—there are a lot of questions you may have, and that's okay! The first thing you need to do is pick a medium. Nothing really compares to good old pen-and-paper journaling, but you can certainly use your laptop or phone as a tool for journaling as well. Whatever works best for you is perfect. However, if you are having trouble picking, consider asking yourself the following questions to help you pick:

- When and where do you plan to journal? Are you someone who might journal on the go, or do you prefer sitting and journaling in the same place?

- How is your handwriting?

- Do you tend to think faster than you can write?

- Is complete and total privacy of the essence?

After that, it is important to try to make journaling an everyday process. It might be hard to get into the swing of it, but journaling every day not only makes journaling easier, but it makes a connection in your brain so that you inherently work through problems as they arise, rather than responding impulsively. In other words, if you journal every single day, it will automatically become a coping mechanism that you use—and a healthy one at that.

In addition, it is a good idea to try to make your journaling practice as convenient as possible. It might be tempting to force yourself to sit down at a desk and journal for an hour a day or something like that, but it is not always feasible. If it works for you and makes you more likely to actually journal, do not be afraid to use a solution that is as simple as the notes app on your phone.

I also recommend refusing to constrict yourself. Write or even draw whatever you see fit, using your journal exactly as you want to. Your journal is yours, and it is only for your eyes. You do not have to journal according to anyone's rules—even mine. Instead, take the time to find what works for you and journal in a way that actually helps you, making it a personal experience that you will want to return to.

Reflective Journaling

There are innumerable ways to journal, but one of the most popular and effective methods for someone with an avoidant attachment style is reflective journaling. You will need the following steps to engage with reflective journaling:

1. Identify your emotions. When you sit down to journal, try to make a concise statement that outlines what you feel, or even spend a few paragraphs exploring what you feel.

2. Consider your triggers. Now, it is time to think about why—why do you feel the emotions you just identified? Try to outline your triggers, whether it was a specific event or even a thought. Write about what you were doing before you felt that emotion come on.

3. Explore your emotions. Next, take some time to explore those emotions, their origin, and what you are thinking about. Make note of what you *want* to do or say in the moment, how you are feeling as a result of what you've experienced, and more.

4. Reflect. Finish by trying to determine what you can learn from the event or experience, and how you can move forward with it.

Do not be afraid to modify those steps, skip around, or otherwise make the practice truly yours. There is far more benefit to personalizing the experience than there is to constraining yourself to steps in a book.

Emotional Awareness Journal Prompts

Before sending you off to the next healing strategy, here are a few emotional awareness journaling prompts you might enjoy:

- Start by identifying and describing the emotions you are currently feeling. Be specific and use descriptive language to capture the nuances of each emotion.

- Reflect on recent events or situations that triggered strong emotional responses. Consider both positive and negative triggers. What about these experiences evoked such emotions?

- Are there recurring emotional patterns in your life? Reflect on whether certain situations consistently trigger specific emotions and how you typically respond to them.

- Write about something or someone you are grateful for. Explore the positive emotions associated with gratitude and how expressing thanks impacts your overall emotional well-being.

- Choose an emotion that you find challenging or difficult. Explore the roots of this emotion, its impact on your thoughts and behaviors, and possible coping strategies.

- Consider any recent changes in your life—whether big or small. Explore how these changes have influenced your emotional landscape and if your emotional responses have shifted.

Remember that journaling is a personal experience. Whether you journal in your phone, in a notebook, or by recording your voice, journaling is an experience that you should personalize and use to help you heal that attachment style.

Avoidant Healing Strategy 3: Connection and Intimacy Building

The next strategy that I have for you is a handful of intimacy and connection-building exercises that you can do alone or with a partner. By working with intimacy and connection-building exercises like the ones we are going to discuss, you can find the ability to bond with others and form more meaningful connections, healing your attachment style in the process.

One way that you can build connection and intimacy is to truly listen when your partner speaks. How often does your partner say something, and it goes in one ear and out the other? Chances are, it is very often. But truly listening to what your partner has to say can be a wonderful way to heighten intimacy between you and someone else. By actively listening—something we will talk about together in a few pages—and asking questions when your partner talks, for instance, your partner will feel heard, you will learn more about them (and yourself), and it will enable you both to resolve conflicts quicker. Plus, if you can communicate wisely, you will not be as likely to respond to situations avoidantly.

It's also a good exercise to spend time expressing gratitude. You and your partner can take turns expressing gratitude for one another, talking about how grateful you are for each other, your relationship generally, and other facets of life. Being grateful is a wonderful way to see that life is not all that bad and that there are positive aspects of life to look forward to. When you and your partner openly communicate about how grateful you are for one another, it opens vulnerability and builds positive emotions.

Something else that you and your partner can do is focus on touch. Physical contact is a major aspect of intimacy for most people, and it goes far beyond sexual contact. Spend time with compassionate physical contact, even if it feels alien or uncomfortable at first. Hugging, holding hands, taking turns massaging one another, or otherwise making minor instances of physical contact can allow you to develop intimacy and connection with your partner. Some activities that I recommend include

- baking together, and taking turns feeding one another

- hugging
- bathing together
- brushing one another's hair
- cuddling
- linking pinkies or holding hands while talking

In addition, you can try connecting with each other through conversational check-ins. When was the last time that you or your partner asked how the other was? It's not something that we ask people we care for a lot, yet sitting down and having a genuine conversation about how the two of you are feeling can be a wonderful bonding opportunity. Even if it feels awkward at first, this can be a great opportunity for healing, vulnerability, and connection.

While intimacy and connection might feel uncomfortable to you, especially at first, it is necessary to work with exercises like the ones I've mentioned in order to truly heal the negative impacts of your attachment style once and for all.

Avoidant Healing Strategy 4: Challenging Negative Core Beliefs

Next, it is important to work on challenging your negative core beliefs. Everyone who has an unhealthy style of attachment has at least a few negative core beliefs that can be identified and changed. And when you do challenge those negative core beliefs, you invite significant healing and growth into your life.

Avoidant attachment creates and facilitates negative core beliefs. This is because avoidant attachment is deeply rooted and causes us to perceive the world around us in such a way that we are unable to grow and heal. Three common types of negative core beliefs of someone with avoidant attachment are

1. Helpless core beliefs. These are core beliefs that center around one's perceived helplessness, and such beliefs are negative because they strip you of responsibility. In other words, when you feel helpless because of your own beliefs, you do not actually try to change your circumstances. This continues to contribute to attachment issues.

2. Worthless core beliefs. These are core beliefs that center around feeling worthless, which is negative because it makes you feel as though you do not deserve better. In turn, you do not put in the work to improve attachment issues or your connection with those around you.

3. Unlovable core beliefs. These are core beliefs that center around your perceived inability to feel loved. When you have such beliefs, it feels impossible to allow anyone to love you, thus worsening avoidant attachment types.

While these beliefs might feel oppressive and quite difficult to change, no negative core belief is permanent. This means that you do have the ability to overcome your negative core beliefs and empower yourself to attach more healthily. But how can you do that?

It begins with identifying your negative beliefs and how they impact you. This is often the hardest part of the process, so allow me to try and help you. The next time you feel something negative, think about why you feel that way. Keep asking yourself "why" until you get to a core idea that can potentially be a core belief. For example, this can look like

- My partner is going to break up with me, so I should break up with them first.

- I feel this way because all of my relationships end badly, so I should not even try.

- I do not deserve to try because I am not worth loving.

This means that your negative core belief in this particular instance is "I am not worth loving." Once you have isolated that negative core thought through questioning your beliefs, you can move into the nitty-gritty of challenging such beliefs.

After that, it is important to try and determine the origin of negative core beliefs. This can be very challenging as well, especially because negative core beliefs can stem from very early childhood. However, by taking the time to weed out some of the potential origins of your negative core beliefs, you can work to resolve them in a more targeted way. Think back to any incident that first made you feel that way, such as feeling like you are not worthy of loving. Once you've isolated one or more events that can be attributed to causing that core belief, you can keep moving.

Now comes another hurdle for you to challenge. You have to accept that those negative thoughts are baseless. Just because you experienced something in childhood does not mean that it is a fixed rule for the rest of your life. An inconsistent caregiver that made you feel unworthy of love has no bearing on how lovable you are as you grow and age. As such, it is important to accept that those negative thoughts are, essentially, without logic and reason.

After that, the last thing that you have to do is replace negative thoughts with positive or even neutral thoughts. Instead of believing that "I am not worthy of love," try shifting that to a viewpoint that is more like "I am as worthy of love as anyone else is." This is a true statement that is more beneficial to your healing and growth.

It might be difficult, but ultimately, challenging your negative core beliefs is crucial. Without this invaluable aspect of healing, you are not going to truly overcome avoidant attachment—you'll just be caught in a cycle of negative thoughts and unhealthy attachment. With the skills you are developing, however, you do not have to let those negative core beliefs have such power over you.

Avoidant Healing Strategy 5: Improve Your Communication

Communication is the final strategy that I have for you. It might seem like common sense, but it is a strategy that packs a lot of punch! There are both positive and negative communication habits that can make or break your relationship with other people, which is why we have to go over both of them in order to truly improve your communication.

Positive Habits to Pick Up

Let's start with the good. There are a ton of positive communication habits that you can pick up in order to improve how you speak with others and the way you attach to them:

- Choosing the right time to bring up a conflict. Sometimes, it can feel easy to explode on someone or lash out, even in a way that is as subtle as distancing yourself. However, there is a time and place for conflict, and by choosing the right time to bring up said conflict, you can have productive discussions.

Usually, the best time for a conflict is when nothing else important is going on and when everyone is in a neutral, private place with a semi-positive mood.

- Being honest in a respectful way. If you feel a certain way about your relationship, good or bad, you can express that. You can openly communicate how you feel with your loved ones, even if the truth that you have to speak is rather harsh. At the same time, it is important to be respectful; remember that others have feelings too, and using "I" statements ("I feel like...," "I do not think...") can help respect those feelings.

- Not hiding your feelings. Hiding your feelings can cause more conflict and reduce the likelihood of working out problems. Plus, hiding feelings is a hallmark sign of avoidance, which means that one of the best ways to overcome avoidance is by being open and proud of your feelings.

- Validating your partner's feelings and perspective. Your feelings are not the only ones that matter, and while you probably know this, it is important to take the time in a conversation to step back and acknowledge the other person's feelings. Even if you disagree, let them know that you understand and respect where they are coming from.

- Staying on topic in conversation. Some of the biggest fights occur as a result of bringing up the past or straying from the point of a conversation. You can prevent this by staying on topic, addressing one concern at a time, and coming to a solution before moving to the next issue(s). Remember that if your partner brought something up, then it is important to them and it should be addressed. It's a matter of respect.

- Taking constructive criticism. Sometimes, your behavior is not going to be healthy or in accordance with what other people need to be happy. If someone genuinely and kindly offers you constructive criticism, it is important to accept and consider that criticism without becoming upset or vindictive.

- Finding compromise. Lastly, remember that it is important to compromise. If you get your way all of the time, then your partner is going to feel unloved, much like you would if you never get your way. As a result, it is important to find compromises to issues within your relationship and talk those compromises through thoroughly.

As you navigate conversations, try finding space for each of these habits. You will not pick them all up right away, but over time, they will be like second nature!

Negative Habits to Let Go Of

Now, it is time to take a look at some negative habits that can be quite destructive in conversation:

- Bottling up your emotions. Bottling your emotions up is never a beneficial thing; doing so can result in a lack of communication. You cannot be mad at your partner for not keeping your feelings in mind if you never communicate said feelings. As a result, it is important to talk about your feelings openly and in a calm manner, even if those feelings are quite explosive.

- Brushing your or your partner's emotions aside. This is a big no-no. Brushing your partner's emotions aside is just as bad as brushing your own aside; either way, both parties are going to feel disrespected, uncared for, and untrusted.

- Using jokes to cover up feelings. While jokes can be an invaluable coping mechanism for some people, there is a time and a place. Using jokes to sugarcoat how you feel can minimize your emotions and prevent them from being fully communicated. At the end of the day, you are your biggest advocate, and you need to stand up for yourself by not minimizing your emotions.

- Being passive-aggressive. Passive aggression is a common tactic that avoidant people use, but it is one that harms both parties and is disrespectful. Do not resort to being passive-aggressive or snappy, even if a conversation is not going the way you want it to.

- Becoming overly defensive. Defensiveness just prevents a conversation from getting anywhere good. If you feel yourself becoming defensive, then it might be a good idea to take a step back and pause, allowing yourself to calm down before continuing the conversation.

- Bringing up unrelated conflict during an argument about a specific topic. This, as I mentioned earlier, is a big way that fights begin. Remain focused; you'll have time to bring up other subjects later on.

- Talking over or ignoring your partner's points. This is plain disrespectful and gives your partner no reason to respect what you have to say.

- Giving your partner the silent treatment after an argument, or to avoid an argument. After an argument, you should have a conversation and come to a solution. Needing a few moments to yourself is one thing, but ignoring your partner after a fight or to avoid a fight is immature and unhelpful.

Communication is a simple yet effective strategy that you can use to heal both your attachment style and your relationship with others. A relationship tainted by poor attachment can certainly be revived with communication, and now you know what needs to change for your communication to improve.

In this chapter, we've explored a wealth of strategies, techniques, and exercises aimed at helping individuals with avoidant attachment styles embark on a journey of healing and transformation. The next chapter focuses on the behavior and traits of disorganized attachment style.

CHAPTER 6

A Deep Dive Into Disorganized Attachment

Attachment style is no different from any other human characteristic. Although we all have a basic need to form close bonds, the way we create them varies.
–Amir Levine & Rachel Heller

In the previous chapters, we talked about two of the most common types of insecure attachment: anxious and avoidant attachment. Now, however, it's time to delve into a third and final insecure attachment style that blends the two previous ones together. Specifically, in this chapter, we will dive into the complexities and intricacies of disorganized attachment. By the end of this chapter, if you're someone who lives with a disorganized attachment style, you will be a master at understanding said style.

This attachment style is one that I know, like the back of my own hand. I didn't always begin from a place of disorganized attachment. In fact, I originally started out with the anxious attachment style many years ago. During that point in my life, I was dating someone with an avoidant form of attachment—obviously making for quite a chaotic situation. It was my first "real" relationship—the truly adult relationship that we always think will last forever and ever.

And while forever didn't happen, that relationship lasted for a long five years. As I said, my partner and I had very conflicting styles of attachment. The relationship left me with a lot of deep-seated wounds, and we were both incredibly insecure in the relationship.

I remember chasing after him constantly, asking for compassion and connection, only to have him turn away. I would beg and plead to solve problems only for him to avoid the issues. I tried to give him my all, but as you know, the "all" of someone who is anxiously attached can be too much for some. Coupled with his avoidance, it was a recipe for disaster.

At the end, he ended up cheating on me, which left an indelible mark on my soul. From that relationship, I began to develop an avoidant attachment style. Meanwhile, I continued searching for my soulmate for the next 10 years, anxiously awaiting compassion only to pull away the second I received it. Because of this hot-and-cold behavior I exhibited, my relationships didn't last long—and it all stemmed from my own fear of abandonment.

This isn't just a tale I've made up for the sake of the book. This is my own true story, and it has resulted in over 10 years of personal struggles. Because of this, it's so important to me that we work on ourselves, heal our inner child, and see genuine progress before jumping into relationships or expecting "true love" to flourish—especially when insecure attachment is thrown into the mix.

Disorganized attachment is a challenge, but I overcame it, and you can too. But before we get into strategies and solutions, let's delve into what exactly this attachment style encompasses.

Characteristics of Disorganized Attachment Style

Understanding disorganized attachment style is important; it blends characteristics of the other two styles, yet it's still a distinctive form of attachment with unique signs, symptoms, and concerns. Now, we're going to explore this final insecure attachment style together.

Signs of Disorganized Attachment

There are many signs that accompany disoAnxiety. Being unsure of how to navigate relationships, who you can trust, and what's going to happen with someone can be a major source of anxiety for a lot of people. Personally, anxiety was one of my biggest mental health concerns before I worked on healing—I always felt on edge!

- Depression. Depression and anxiety are often intertwined, and feeling like you can't handle relationships can be a source of depression as well.
- Social withdrawal. Because there are significant issues when it comes to socializing, connection, and more,

many people with a disorganized attachment style will actively choose to isolate themselves. For others, this is a more unconscious shift.

- Substance abuse. People who attach in a disorganized way are prone to substance abuse to cope with the symptoms and impacts of their attachment style.

And that's only the start of it. Mental health concerns often plague those with insecure attachment styles, and I can safely say that those with disorganized attachment get the brunt of it due to the on-and-off quality of symptoms.

One final yet major sign of disorganized attachment is impulsive behavior or "acting out." Someone with this attachment style might make impulsive decisions pertaining to their relationship, make risky choices in their life to compensate for lacking in other areas, and more. This can get someone with this attachment style into a lot of trouble with others.

Disorganized Attachment Triggers

Like the other two attachment styles, disorganized attachment has a unique set of triggers that contribute to how strongly the symptoms of attachment show. Some of those triggers can include

- Signs of rejection, distance, or abandonment. This can look like someone not responding to texts, coming home late, or seeming distant. This can trigger the more intimacy-craving aspects of this attachment style, making someone feel unloved and uncared for. As a result, someone who is attached in a disorganized way will either try to cling to the person harder, or they will isolate altogether so that they can avoid the "inevitable" downfall of a relationship.

- Inconsistent behavior. Someone who is loving one moment and then distant the next can massively trigger disorganized attachment symptoms. Such behavior is very reminiscent of hot and cold behavior from childhood and caregivers, which means that it can trigger anger, frustration, or fear within someone with this attachment style.

- Avoidant behaviors. For someone who struggles with disorganized attachment, it can be very triggering to see other people try to avoid how we feel. Avoidant behaviors like shutting down a conversation, walking away from a conversation, or giving us the silent treatment can trigger the signs that are associated with disorganized attachment.

- Intimacy-seeking behaviors. Someone with a disorganized style of attachment can also be triggered by intimacy-seeking actions. Remember that the disorganized attachment style sort of intertwines anxious and avoidant attachment. Therefore, it can be simple for someone with a disorganized attachment style to be triggered by avoidance and intimacy. Behaviors like future plans, romantic gestures, emotional needs, and vulnerability can trigger the symptoms of disorganized attachment.

- Criticism. Whether real or imagined, criticism can make someone with a disorganized attachment style feel unwanted and unloved. This, in turn, results in disorganized attachment symptoms flaring up. Someone with this attachment style can, when criticized, shut down and push others away.

- Loss of control. When someone with a disorganized attachment style feels out of control in a relationship, they're more likely to experience the signs of their attachment style. They may do what they can to retain that control, even if it includes trying to control their partner in various ways.

- Authority figures. Because someone with this attachment style had a very unreliable connection with authority figures—specifically their caregivers, imposed authority or figures of authority in and outside of a relationship can be a trigger.

- Reminders of past trauma. When incidents come up that can be reminiscent of past trauma, it is easy for someone with this attachment style to become triggered.

Understanding these triggers is your gateway to overcoming them *and* your symptoms. But for now, let's look at what disorganized attachment looks like in the context of a relationship.

The Disorganized Partner in Relationships

It might be the case that you have a partner with a disorganized attachment style, or you're just interested in what such an attachment style looks like in a relationship. Either way, it's time to really explore what a disorganized partner looks like within a relationship.

Naturally, dating someone with a disorganized style of attachment can pose significant issues for a relationship. If your partner has this style of attachment, or if you're wondering the extent of the implications of your attachment style, then it's time for us to really delve into the world of disorganized attachment within the context of a relationship.

In a relationship, many unique challenges can arise due to disorganized attachment. For example, those who date someone with a disorganized style of attachment frequently report mixed signals. This means that one moment, their partner might be very clingy, craving affection and reassurance to no end. Then, the next moment, that same person will be distant and cold, even snappy, if interacted with. Such inconsistent behavior and mixed signals can result in relationship conflict, including confusion in a securely attached partner or mistreatment. This means that the hot-and-cold behavior of someone with a disorganized attachment style can, at times, be just as harrowing as the childhood treatment they received.

Something else that frequently comes up in relationships where one partner is disorganized is trust issues. Someone with a disorganized style of attachment is no stranger to rampant trust issues, but those show up uniquely within the framework of a relationship. For example, someone with a disorganized style of attachment and trust issues might be overly suspicious, even without evidence. This can also involve jumping to conclusions based on a similar lack of evidence. This can transform from you hanging out with a friend into a situation where your disorganized partner believes you to be cheating and leaving them. What's more, this cycle of distrust can pair with hot-and-cold treatment for a true mess of misunderstandings and overcomplications.

In addition, trying to have an argument or even a plain constructive conversation can feel like an uphill battle when it comes to someone with a disorganized style of attachment. Most commonly, people with this attachment style will shut down or go numb during arguments. This is usually a trauma response that mostly pertains to the fact that conflict hasn't gone well for them in the past; however, that doesn't make it any easier to deal with in your current relationship. Because of this tendency, it can be hard to feel cared for, supported, or heard in a relationship—conflicts often go unresolved due to this common coping tactic.

Relationship sabotage isn't uncommon for someone with a disorganized attachment style either. Someone who has such an insecure attachment style will intentionally try to find reasons to break off the relationship. They will spend time digging for signs of lying, disloyal behavior, and other issues within a relationship—often creating new issues along the way. Or, someone with this attachment style will endeavor to force their partner to end the relationship. They might do something offensive, abrasive, or hurtful in order to get their partner to end the relationship, giving them an "out," so to speak. Of course, no relationship can thrive in this state or condition.

Beyond that, people with a disorganized attachment style will usually pick partners who are unsuitable for this. This is one of the many reasons that insecurely attached people never break out of the cycle—they intentionally choose people who will help fulfill or repeat the cycle. And this extends far beyond simply picking incompatible partners. Someone with a disorganized style of attachment may intentionally seek out partners who exhibit abusive or controlling tendencies, knowing that this will either make them comfortable within their attachment or give them a reason to be distant or play the victim. Naturally, this isn't going to land someone in a healthy relationship either because they intentionally sought out something bad for them.

And it doesn't end there—someone with this style of attachment isn't afraid to create unhealthy dynamics within an otherwise healthy relationship. They might pick fights, intentionally hurt their partner in some way, or otherwise behave in unacceptable ways in order to create that unhealthy dynamic that they're so familiar with. This clearly has an impact on their partner as well. If someone with a disorganized style is dating someone with a similar insecure style of attachment, for instance, it can trap them both in the cycle; if the partner of someone with this attachment style is secure, it can result in irrevocable damage to the secure individual.

At the end of the day, there are a lot of unique facets and challenges that arise when you experience a relationship with disorganized attachment. Overwhelmingly, these effects are negative, which is why working to overcome this style of attachment is so important—both for you and for any future relationships you might encounter.

With this understanding of disorganized attachment, you can identify where your triggers come from and how they impact your relationships—among other things. Now, it's time to jump into solutions that can help you break free from the constraints of your attachment style. Remember that love is never simple, and disorganized attachment patterns can be nuanced. The next chapter explores strategies for moving from disorganized tendencies to secure connections, to help you create the lasting, fulfilling relationships you desire.

CHAPTER 7

Finding Harmony in Disorganized Attachment

Disorganized folks are often emotionally dysregulated, dealing with sudden shifts in arousal, or dissociated and checked out. Since they are prone to the most disturbance, reestablishing a fundamental sense of regulation and relative safety are the most important things for people with this attachment style.

–Diane Poole Heller

It is possible to find harmony in relationships when you're starting from a disorganized style of attachment. This is something that I know first-hand. At first, my journey to growth was complicated and a bit stressful, but I made the active decision to commit to personal growth and attachment transformation. Over time, making this progress became second nature to me, and it invited so much positivity into my life.

For example, I noticed that my interactions with other people—even people I never dated nor would date, like friends and family—tended to be stronger. When someone mentioned hanging out with another friend, my first thoughts were along the lines of how nice, rather than that means they don't want to hang out with me! Beyond that, my love life improved dramatically. For the first time in my life, I felt like I was able to see and enforce my worth within a relationship. Anxiety was the last thing on my mind.

So, how did I do it? It wasn't always easy, and there wasn't one simple solution—rather, I used a lot of different strategies to help me along my journey. Notably, I started journaling. One professional said that I should write letters to myself and express how I really feel about myself—no matter how cruel those letters may be. She asked me to write one every single day, which at first seemed like overkill. However, after just a week of doing so, I noticed something.

My letters began to be more understanding, more compassionate, and more kind. Reading back over my older letters, I want to cry at how much anger I held in my heart for myself. But it's because of that starting point that I am where I am today.

And my dedication to growth didn't end there. After seeing how much my self-compassion lacked, I made it a point to engage in acts of self-compassion every single day. When I found myself being overly critical, I talked to myself about why I did what I did and what I could improve next time—replacing my usual habit of berating myself. I also took the time to heighten my personal intimacy with myself through self-care.

There are so many other things that I tried as well, and we're going to talk about them in this chapter. The point is that truly transforming your attachment style comes from dedication and effort. It's less about the methods you use and more about what you put into them—everything you need to heal is already inside of you.

With all of that being said, this chapter centers itself around providing you with a comprehensive set of tools and strategies for coping with disorganized attachment—all of which were instrumental in my own healing process. This chapter is your gateway to harnessing true, compassionate relationships and transforming your attachment style, so let's not delay and get started now!

Practice Self-Compassion: Tame Your Inner Critic

One of the most valuable tools you can hone when it comes to overcoming disorganized attachment is a mindset of self-compassion. Self-compassion is a skill that not everyone has, but that everyone can develop. But what does it mean to be compassionate toward yourself, exactly?

In short, self-compassion involves treating yourself with kindness and understanding. It's a mindset where, rather than berating yourself for mistakes or shortcomings, you use obstacles and challenges as an opportunity to grow. Fundamentally, people who are self-compassionate encourage themselves. They recognize their humanity and understand that they're not infallible. This leads to being nicer to yourself and treating yourself in a way that isn't cruel or unrealistic. Self-compassion is self-kindness.

Self-compassion can look like different things. Someone's definition of self-compassion can be forcing themselves to make dinner even when they don't want to, knowing that they really need the nutrition. Someone else's definition of self-compassion can look like a lazy day in bed when the world is too much. And everything in between those two scenarios can be self-compassion; it depends on what you personally need and your treatment of challenges in your life. My self-compassion is going to look different from yours.

Benefits of Self-Compassion

When I mention self-compassion, many people ask me why they should bother with it. What, really, is the difference between a mindset of self-compassion and a mindset of non-compassion? As it turns out, there is a staggering difference and numerous benefits that accompany being compassionate toward oneself. Just a few of those benefits include

- Mental and emotional well-being. Those who are kinder to themselves tend to be less susceptible to depression, anxiety, and other mental health issues. Beyond that, those who are compassionate toward themselves have higher self-esteem, are happier people, and can even extend compassion to others more naturally. As a result, stronger bonds are formed—ones that make you feel better and more secure.

- Physical health. Self-compassion can, believe it or not, improve your physical health too! When you're happier, you are also less likely to be in pain, suffer from the physical effects of stress, and more. And beyond that, those with high levels of self-compassion usually take better care of themselves, eating healthier foods, drinking more water, and otherwise engaging with basic forms of self-care.

- A growth mindset. People who have a growth mindset believe that they can change their skills, traits, and habits to make themselves a better person. This is opposed to a fixed mindset, where one believes that they are stuck with the traits and skills they have. Self-compassion and a growth mindset are linked, meaning that one is likely to produce the other. That means that when you engage with self-compassion, you also allow yourself to grow.

And that's far from all of the benefits that accompany a self-compassionate attitude, but for now, we'll stick to the big three. The grand takeaway is that self-compassion is certainly worth it and is far better to have than a non-compassionate attitude toward yourself!

Components of Self-Compassion

I mentioned that being kind to yourself is a main component of self-compassion, but there are more components that intersect in order to make you truly compassionate toward yourself! By understanding the different components that come into play with self-compassion, you can heighten your ability to extend that compassion to yourself.

Most fundamentally, self-compassion involves self-kindness. You can't truly be compassionate toward yourself if you're not kind to yourself as well. Specifically, this means treating yourself like you would treat your best friend or someone you love dearly. You wouldn't admonish them for a mistake, nor would you tell them that they are unworthy of loving and being loved. Therefore, you shouldn't treat yourself in such a way, either. Kindness is the hallmark of compassion because when you really understand someone, you're going to be kind to them. This is where common humanity comes into play.

Recognizing your common humanity is another important part of self-compassion. When you recognize the humanity of someone, it's easier to be compassionate toward them—and that includes you. Sometimes, when we deal with complex problems like disorganized attachment, it can be easy to feel like we aren't like others—we don't love like other people, deserve what other people deserve, or act as they act. This feeling can make us wonder why we should be compassionate to ourselves. However, when you learn to recognize that you're a part of humanity just like everyone else, you have the realization that there is no reason to treat yourself harshly—you gain nothing in doing so.

The final aspect of self-compassion is mindfulness. Someone who is mindful is aware of their surroundings, as well as the internal workings of their mind. This means that they are self-aware, understanding why they feel certain ways and the motives behind their actions. This means that by honing your mindfulness skills, you can come to understand yourself better—which, in turn, enables you to be more compassionate.

How to Be Self-Compassionate

Now that you have a firm understanding of what self-compassion is, why it matters, and the components that make up a strong sense of self-compassion, you are probably wondering what exactly you can do in order to enable yourself to be more compassionate. While there are hundreds of methods for enhancing your levels of self-compassion, we are going to focus on four of my favorite methods—and the most common methods—for enhancing self-compassion.

First, you have to think about physical touch. Many people do not think about how harsh they are being when they scratch, hit, or otherwise physically interact with their own bodies. It can be rather easy to allow physical touch to enter the back of your mind, because, after all, why bother with gentleness when it is only you? However, being mindful of physical touch can be one of the best ways to improve your levels of compassion toward yourself. Some ways that you can physically enhance self-compassion through touch include

- Applying lotion thoughtfully. After you wash your hands or finish showering, spend some time thoughtfully massaging lotion into your hands, legs, or other parts of your body. This will help you understand how to provide gentle, compassionate touches for yourself, helping you find more love and respect for yourself and your body.

- Brushing your own hair. Take the time to mindfully brush through your hair carefully and gently, appreciating each stroke as you do. We often neglect to consider our own beauty, but there's beauty in everyone. Now is the perfect time to notice that.

- Exfoliating in the bath. Exfoliating your arms, legs, shoulders, and back can be a good way to leave yourself feeling good after a bath. It can also be a magnificent way to tie in physical touch as a form of self-compassion.

And more: If you notice, all of these physical touches are also forms of physical self-care; physical self-care is generally a wonderful way to improve your self-compassion!

Something else that you can do to improve your self-compassion skills is to work on your emotional intelligence. Oftentimes, we are mean to ourselves because we lack understanding or nuance in the way we perceive emotions.

Therefore, working on your emotional intelligence and agility can be a lifesaver when it comes to self-compassion. Try to pay attention to how you feel, what you think about your feelings, and more, and respond to them how you would a friend rather than how you would typically respond to yourself.

Beyond that, you have the opportunity to practice mindfulness on its own in order to enhance your relationship with yourself. Mindfulness simply involves taking note of your present surroundings, intentions, thoughts, and awareness. While some people can find this to be a rather elusive practice, all it takes is a few minutes and ease.

Try it right now: Sit and think about what's going on around you, noticing everything without judgment. Try to do this for five minutes. At the end of those five minutes, guess what? You will have practiced mindfulness! Over time and with consistency, such a practice has stellar benefits for self-compassion and nonjudgmental awareness of your emotions.

My last suggestion is to work on externalizing your inner critic. We are going to discuss the inner critic on its own momentarily, but the inner critic does play a role in our self-compassion. You likely know your inner critic well; they are the voice in the back of your mind that tears you down, tells you you do not deserve something, or will never live up to a standard. By getting the inner critic out of your head, you can truly realize how ridiculous and preposterous some of their cries are.

Self-compassion is not built overnight, but with these three tools—and every other tool you can find along the way—the journey to self-compassion has never been easier. Remember that consistency is the key to a strong level of self-compassion, so do not give up if things get hard!

Silencing a Harsh Inner Critic

In all of my experience, I have never met someone who began the healing process free of an inner critic. Most people, if not all people, have an inner critic; however, some people allow their inner critic more power than others. In order to transform your attachment style, it is necessary to silence that inner critic because they are the source of most of your doubt.

Your inner critic can exist for a few different reasons. For example, trauma can make an inner critic harsher and, therefore, more present. If you had a caregiver who was harsh in their judgment of you, for instance, that can really stick and make it easy to similarly berate yourself. A strong yet negative inner critic can also come from low self-esteem, your attachment style itself, and more sources.

Silencing a harsh inner critic is vital to overpowering a disorganized style of attachment. This is because your inner critic can, when negative, really reinforce those unhealthy and unhelpful thoughts that contribute to disorganized attachment. Thoughts that you are not worthy or good enough, or even insecurities about whether your partner likes you, can all be signs of a harsh inner critic worsening your attachment issues. Thus, managing your inner critic can be a gateway to overcoming your attachment-related struggles.

Tips for Silencing Them

So, how do you silence a harsh inner critic? One way that you can do so is through affirmations—ones that affirm that you are a lovable, worthy, and wonderful person. This is where self-compassion can come into play yet again because self-compassion-centered affirmations can help with inner critic concerns. Some affirmations you might want to use include

1. I release self-doubt and embrace my inner strength, knowing that I am capable and worthy.

2. My mistakes are opportunities for growth, and I am learning and evolving every day.

3. I am not defined by my past; I am creating a positive and empowered present and future.

4. I trust in my abilities and believe in my unique talents. I am enough just as I am.

5. I let go of perfectionism and embrace the beauty of my imperfections. They make me who I am.

6. I choose self-compassion over self-criticism, recognizing that I am a work in progress.

7. My worth is not determined by the opinions of others. I am valuable just by being myself.

8. I release the need for validation from others. I validate and appreciate myself.

9. I replace negative thoughts with positive affirmations, creating a mindset of empowerment and positivity.

10. I am the author of my own story, and I choose to write a narrative filled with self-love and confidence.

In addition, you can try naming your critic. It might feel weird to talk to a named person who only exists in your mind, but when you name your inner critic, it becomes easier to separate their devious interactions from who you are as a person. Rather than "I know I'm a bad person," it can easily become "Yeah, Kyle's babbling about me being a bad person again." This distinction can be powerful in remedying a tendency to allow the inner critic to take control.

Furthermore, I always recommend that people assess the evidence in favor of disproving a negative thought from the inner critic. You might think that you are not worthy of love, but really, what evidence supports that line of thinking? Someone treating you poorly in the past by no means indicates that you are not worthy of love, so unless you can come up with viable evidence, this is powerful for shutting the inner critic down.

Plus, if you do come up with something "viable," you can use it as an opportunity to grow. You might think, for example, that you are not worthy of love because you did this, that, and the other to your partner intentionally to hurt them. This does not mean that you are unworthy, though; rather, it highlights an opportunity that you can use to grow and change from the confines of your attachment style. Why did you do those things in the first place? Chances are, there was something underlying to be worked on!

At the end of the day, your inner critic can go from your strongest hater to your best friend if you know how to silence their harsh words and transform them into a constructive voice. And beyond that, this can be instrumental in helping you master a secure attachment style and everything that comes along with it.

Learn to Communicate Your Feelings

Someone with a disorganized style of attachment can often struggle with communicating how they feel. At the same time, overcoming communication complexities and mastering strong emotional communication is vital for a secure style of attachment. Some of the reasons you might be uncomfortable or unable to communicate your feelings include:

- Vulnerability. Vulnerability is a major point of contention for someone with a disorganized style of attachment. Sharing emotions can be a very vulnerable thing, and for someone to whom that vulnerability is discomforting, sharing emotions can feel all but impossible. As such, someone with disorganized attachment issues might feel a strong blockage when it comes to sharing emotions.

- Lack of understanding. Sometimes, we do not understand our own emotions, and more often, we do not understand how to convey them. Finding the ability to communicate your feelings can be as simple as gaining skills and strategies for emotional communication, as those skills are not always second nature.

- Trauma and fear. In the past, you might have been in a situation where sharing your emotions was not safe. A caregiver, past partner, or even friend might have been less than receptive when it came to sharing your emotions, which makes you feel anxious about sharing them, even with someone who you have no reason to expect would respond poorly.

- Anger and overwhelm. Sharing emotions can be an experience that stirs up more emotions. One of the main issues you might experience when it comes to sharing your emotions is feeling angry or overwhelmed while doing so, preventing effective communication.

At the same time, being unable to share your emotions can impact your partner and your relationship as a whole. Being able to share your emotions is a valuable component of intimacy. When you do not trust your partner enough to learn to share your emotions, it can result in shallow and unfulfilling relationships. Your partner may then feel uncomfortable sharing their emotions with you, or they may feel unappreciated or untrustworthy within the scope of your relationship.

All of this means that the solution is clear. You have to work on your capacity to share your emotions in order to break free from attachment-based issues. But of course, I cannot just say, "You have to share your emotions" and expect that to solve all of your problems; let's discuss some ways that you can work on sharing your emotions with your partner!

Tips for Sharing Emotions

There are so many ways that you can work to share your emotions, even making it an overwhelming feat at times. I'm going to focus on sharing just a few of the best ways to share emotions and form the skill with you, empowering you in the skill of emotional expression without making it too complicated.

When it boils down to it, sharing your emotions can really be condensed into a three-step process. And while that three-step process might take some effort, dedication, and getting used to, it is an effective process that I have used myself and had a lot of success with, and others have too.

The first step involved in sharing your emotions is accepting your emotions. Once upon a time, I used to condemn my emotions. When I felt upset and like I deserved more from a situation, I would tell myself to suck it up and get over it. I felt like I did not have the right to express those emotions, and that, on some level, I did *not* deserve more. Do you know what happened as a result? Those emotions became stronger, and they entangled themselves with frustration, anger, and despair. Nothing was ever resolved by rejecting my emotions.

You do not do yourself any favors by rejecting your emotions like that; in fact, doing so can make the emotions stronger and more difficult to tolerate. You have to accept your emotions, whether you like them or not, if you hope to be happy, secure, and otherwise able to communicate your emotions. The best way to accept your emotions is to tell yourself that they are neither right nor wrong. You feel how you feel; it is the resultant behavior and way that you respond to those emotions that make something right or wrong, bad or good. Once you have accepted that, you can move to step two!

The second step in the process is describing your emotions. This is the biggest hurdle for most people, as it can be quite challenging to find words we deem just right for explaining how we feel. Before trying to express the emotion you are having, try to just write it out. Write down everything you are feeling, no matter how confusing it might be. This not only serves to get out the initial outburst of emotions, but it also helps with identifying what is the most important to communicate about the emotion. From your writing, try to condense what you feel into one or two sentences. Start your communication there and see where it goes.

You are probably hoping that the third step is some miracle solution that saves the day; unfortunately, and also, fortunately, the third step is far simpler: practice. Take the time to practice saying how you feel, even if you have to say it in small steps. It might feel strange, but use statements starting with the word "I" and build up how you feel. It's okay to look at your partner and say, "I feel sad. I feel disconnected from you. I feel unworthy of love," and slowly build your emotional expression that way.

Consistency is the most important aspect of learning to express your emotions. Right now, it might feel like rolling a massive boulder uphill, but once you get that boulder to the top, it is all smooth sailing. Take the time to try and express your emotions clearly. Even if it is scary, it will soon feel as natural as blinking!

Activity: Self-Compassion Exercises

Before sending you off to the next and final chapter of our journey together, I wanted to provide you with some additional activities for self-compassion. Below are three additional self-compassion exercises you can engage with to boost the role of compassion in your life. Please make it a point to give each one a chance!

1. Compassion break. Overworking or stressing yourself out is not going to be a helpful part of your recovery; in fact, it can do quite the opposite. At least once a day, try to take a mental step back from whatever you are doing and give yourself a compassion break. If you are stressed, let yourself know that you are doing the best you can. Try to acknowledge doubts and worries without judgment during this time.

2. Supportive touch. Supportive touch, life self-massaging your hands, massaging lotion into your skin, or otherwise engaging with compassionate touch can be helpful as well.

3. Self-compassion journal. Journaling about your experience with self-compassion can be helpful too. Make a note of common traps you find yourself in when it comes to lacking compassion for yourself, and then write down how you can overcome those struggles with a compassionate outlook.

The journey to navigating disorganized attachment may be challenging, but it is not insurmountable. With the insights gained in this chapter, you are better prepared to navigate the complexities of disorganized attachment and foster greater understanding and empathy in your relationships. In the next chapter, we will dive into the world of secure attachment—a relationship style marked by trust, emotional intimacy, and resilience.

CHAPTER 8

Experiencing the Bliss of Secure Love

As we familiarize ourselves more with secure attachment, our relationships become easier and more rewarding—we're less reactive, more receptive, more available for connection, healthier, and much more likely to bring out the securely attached tendencies in others. –Diane Poole Heller

Throughout the last seven chapters, we have covered everything you need to know about the three forms of insecure attachment. By now, therefore, you are familiar with your style and what it takes to overcome your particular form of attachment. That is such a wonderful way to dive into this journey, but now, you might be wondering what does secure attachment look like? And then, what can you do to wholly and truly embrace a secure form of attachment within relationships?

This chapter is dedicated to helping you understand secure attachment and everything you need to finish making this attachment style your own. This means that you are about to explore the characteristics and superpowers of secure attachment, the communication skills any securely attached partner needs, and several other tips for nurturing a secure attachment style. Buckle up, because we are about to journey through the home stretch of your attachment style healing.

Understanding the Secure Attachment Style

When you began reading this book, you started with an insecure style of attachment. This means that you have never really gotten a close look at how a secure form of attachment manifests, nor the superpowers that really make it such a gem when it comes to dating, friendships, and more general social interactions. What exactly characterizes a secure style of attachment?

Characteristics of Secure Attachment in Adults

There are a lot of characteristics that make up secure attachment. For example, someone who is securely attached suffers from far less anxiety than someone with an insecure style of attachment. Neither a missed call nor intimacy (nor anything in between) is a source of anxiety for someone who is securely attached. When worries do come up, they are clearly expressed, communicated, and resolved in no time—resulting in a much happier partnership overall.

In addition, those with a secure attachment style are less likely to be hostile or prone to anger. One main facet of secure attachment is strong emotional intelligence, which means that someone with this attachment style can not only communicate better but they can control their emotions during that communication as well. As a result, lashing out, impulsive statements and accusations, and more are left out of the equation.

Mindset comes into play as well. A positive mindset is not uncommon for someone who is securely attached. Someone with this form of attachment has a positive and realistic outlook on their relationships, and they view themselves in a positive manner, too. And when you have strong self-esteem within a relationship, you are less susceptible to insecurity and conflict as a result. For securely attached individuals, loving themselves and seeing their inherent worth within a dynamic is only natural.

Similarly, securely attached individuals also have a positive view of other people. In a relationship, securely attached people can see the positives of others. If someone comes home late or misses a date, for example, a securely attached person will assume that they meant no harm and then have a constructive conversation about it. In contrast, an insecurely attached person in the same situation might default to assuming the worst—creating anxiety, conflict, and disharmony all the while.

Beyond that, someone with this form of attachment is comfortable with intimacy. Being emotionally, physically, and spiritually close to someone is not a frightening experience. Rather, it is an opportunity for expressing love, connection, and personal emotions for one another. If someone who is securely attached senses a problem or conflict within their intimate relationships, they will ask their partner if they feel the same, try to figure out what is going on, and come to a solution that genuinely benefits all parties. This is a major step up from how insecurely attached individuals tend to behave in the same scenario.

Boundary setting is another positive aspect of a secure attachment style. Many people with insecure attachment styles will not set firm boundaries or will set boundaries that are entirely isolating. On the other hand, someone with a secure form of attachment will be able to set and enforce strong boundaries that are just that—boundaries and not limitations. What's more, is that securely attached people can actually communicate those boundaries as opposed to expecting people to know them or allowing their boundaries to be negated.

If you have ever wished that you were more independent, then you are in luck—a secure attachment style is also known to make individuals far more self-sufficient. The over-reliance on a partner that is characteristic of someone with an insecure attachment style is not present for those who are secure. Moreover, someone with a secure attachment style is comfortable asking for help when they need it. In combination, this means that there is a confident and secure balance of reliance and independence for both partners as far as secure attachment goes—a stark contrast to what insecure relationships look like.

Also, someone with a secure style of attachment can trust others who are deserving of trust without complication. Trust issues are rampant for those who struggle with an insecure style of attachment; however, those who are securely attached maintain the ability to not only identify trustworthy individuals but put their trust and faith in those people. This means that, for example, if their partner says they are staying late at work, they believe them (as opposed to being suspicious).

Another benefit of a secure attachment style is that people often feel comfortable in their company. In other words, if you have a secure form of attachment, people are going to enjoy spending time around you more often. This, in turn, empowers stronger connections, better quality time, and overall, more secure ties with others. You do not have to worry about people leaving due to excessive clinginess or cold behavior, for example, because secure attachment is "just right."

Furthermore, those who are securely attached also maintain a wonderful sense of emotional balance. People who deal with insecure attachment often struggle with emotional dysregulation; one moment, anger takes hold, only to be replaced by intense sadness or fear the next moment. Secure people, on the other hand, can control and understand their emotions far better. Emotions do not rapidly change from one moment to the next, and those emotions do not impact other people in such severe ways as they do when it comes to insecure attachment.

And those with secure attachment can actually help those around them improve their emotional regulation and attachment style too. This is why many people say that an insecurely attached individual with a growth mindset can find that growth by dating someone with a secure form of attachment.

In all, someone with a secure attachment style is able to secure relationships, form connections, and otherwise exist cohesively and in harmony with others. When you have a secure form of attachment, the issues enforced by insecure attachment melt away, being replaced with strong ties and conflict resolution. And these benefits are not even all that accompany secure attachment!

The Superpowers of Secure Attachment

In addition to plain old benefits, secure attachment also comes along with superpowers! Such superpowers can help you navigate relationships, overcome struggles, and even help others navigate their own journey. Let's take a look at some of the superpowers of someone who has a secure form of attachment!

First, someone with secure attachment has the superpower of being equipped to handle conflict in a relationship. Those with insecure attachment styles handle conflict in varying ways, but none of those ways tend to be healthy. This is far from the case for someone with secure attachment. With the power of secure attachment, one can

- Discuss how they feel in the context of a relationship, and understand how their partner feels.

- Communicate issues, shortcomings, and conflicts with ease, and collaborate on an effective solution.

- Overcome and navigate insecurity, differing desires, and similar relationship conflicts.

And more. Secure attachment makes it so easy to maintain healthy relationships due to the strong ability to handle conflict—and avoid creating more conflict all the while.

Moreover, someone with secure attachment has the superpower of being warm and open with their partner. As you know, not everyone has the ability to form such a strong, vulnerable connection with their partner. But to someone who securely attaches to others, warmth and openness are only natural. You will not find hot-and-cold behavior, a lack of vulnerability, or anything of the like in a securely attached relationship!

Another superpower of secure attachment is comfort with oneself. This means that securely attached people can truly be themselves in a relationship. They do not have to put on a mask to make others like them more, nor do they have to compromise their needs and desires for the sake of a relationship. Instead, they find compatible partners with whom they can truly and irrevocably be and express themselves.

In addition, someone with this attachment style is truly super when it comes to asking for and giving support. Without hesitation, securely attached people can ask to be supported without worrying about backlash, and they can also offer support to their partner without being overwhelmed by the feeling of being needed. This certainly is different from what you would be used to with an anxious, avoidant, or disorganized style of attachment. As a result, both partners in a relationship feel that their needs are met comfortably—lowering the need for insecurity, anxiety, or conflict.

Something else that sets those with a secure attachment style apart from those with insecure attachment is that secure individuals do not really tend to jump into relationships. Someone with an insecure form of attachment might find it easy to jump into different relationships impulsively; they might even seek out relationships that they know are incompatible with their needs. However, someone who has a secure attachment style is not afraid to wait for "the one." They do not rush into relationships, and they have happier and longer relationships as a result.

Additionally, secure individuals have the superpower of understanding when and if a relationship simply is not going to work. Anxious and disorganized individuals, in particular, have a hard time discerning when enough is enough. They will try to make a relationship work even when it has obviously hit a dead end, which can overcomplicate things dramatically. In contrast, someone who has secure attachment superpowers can understand if a relationship is not going to work. They also know how to securely and reasonably end said relationships.

With all of that being said, there are no disadvantages to being securely attached. Health, happiness, and positivity are abundant when you have a healthy style of attachment, making it a wonderful way to transform yourself and grow. Throughout the book, you have learned ways to overcome your insecure attachment; now, however, it is time to take a look at reinforcing a *secure* form of attachment!

Communication for Secure Attachment

Communication is one of the most invaluable skills when it comes to securely attaching to those around you. Communication not only helps with conflict resolution but it has been known to heighten the satisfaction individuals derive from a relationship. With that being said, in order to harness communication within a relationship, it is important to explore various communication-related skills. That's just what we are going to do right now. When it comes to improving the communication that you have with your partner, you can use skills like mindfulness, active listening, honesty, and more to see results.

Mindfulness as a Communication Skill

When many people think of meditation, the idea of meditation as a communication skill does not often come to mind. They tend to view meditation as more of a self-improvement task, which it certainly can be. However, mindfulness can be beneficial for communication in two different ways.

On one hand, your personal meditation practice can enhance your ability to communicate. When you spend time engaging in mindfulness tactics, such as meditation, you improve your ability to understand yourself and the world around you. This means that when you go to communicate with others, you have the ability to do so with improved levels of maturity, logic, reason, and empathy. Similarly, if your partner develops a mindfulness practice, too, then communication back and forth can improve tenfold.

On the other hand, mindfulness can play an active role in conversations as they happen. When you are actively having a conversation, you can choose to initiate mindfulness. This can look like actively paying attention to what someone is saying to you, or paying attention to your responses to what they say—or even what you have to say. When you engage in a conversation mindfully, it is far more likely for both partners to truly feel heard, conflicts to be resolved, and ultimately, greater satisfaction to result.

Therefore, mindfulness can serve as an invaluable communication skill. If you are looking to improve your ability to talk or solve problems with your partner, a bit of mindfulness will do both of you some good!

Seek Understanding and Make It a Priority

Next, it is important that you seek understanding within communication to truly make a difference when it comes to your relationship. How often do you listen to your partner, but only to get your turn to speak, not to understand their point at all? Chances are, you do this often, and it is time to change that. In order to maintain strong communication, you have to make understanding a priority. But what does this look like?

One way that you can make understanding a priority within the communication of your relationship is to ask questions. If you are not sure that you understand or need some elaboration, do not be afraid to ask your partner a question. Now, keep in mind that these questions should be positive and well-meaning. Some insecurely attached people will ask questions like "So, you do not care about how I feel?" to try and guilt trip their partner. It's best to avoid such passive-aggressive comments.

You can also make it a point to understand your partner by restating what they said. But do not just state it as if you'd had the thought, as that seems like you were not listening and just happened to make the same points. Instead, start with something like "From what I understand, you think/feel/want..." and work from there. Expressing your take on their thoughts can help work out any misunderstandings between the two of you.

If all else fails, just ask your partner what they need from you in order to feel understood. If your partner knows what they need and can tell you, then chances are, less confusion will ruminate within the relationship. Just remember that kind understanding is the goal!

Speak Clearly and With Clarity

When communicating with your partner, it is also important that you strive to communicate in a way that gets your point across. Try to avoid stumbling over your words and restating your thoughts over and over, and instead, focus on making logical statements that express your feelings, concerns, or needs.

This might feel difficult at first, but it is just another one of those things that you have to practice. If you need a minute to compose your thoughts, even in the middle of a conversation or conflict, kindly let your partner know. A secure and supportive partner will be happy to allow you that time because the goal is to come to a constructive solution, not to keep arguing.

Practice Active Listening

There is a difference between listening and active listening. While you can hear the words someone else is saying, you might find that after the fact, you are not really sure what they said after all. This is something that causes a lot of conflict and misunderstanding in relationships, so it is best to nip this bad habit in the bud right now.

Active listening involves really paying attention to, and understanding, the words that someone is saying. Rather than listening to them so you can get to your turn to speak, active listening is done to facilitate understanding, show that you care about your loved one, and more. Some ways that you can work to listen actively include

- Look at your partner and make eye contact while they are speaking. If your partner is talking to you and you are on your phone or even just looking at the floor, it can be hard to actually understand and retain what they are trying to say.

- Pay attention to nonverbal cues, including facial expressions and body language. Our words are not the only way that we can communicate, after all.

- Listen without judgment, and refrain from assuming or jumping to conclusions. Judgmental listening or assuming that you know how someone's thought or sentence will end is a poor way to listen and show respect for your partner.

- Avoid planning what to say next. When you spend your mental energy trying to come up with your next point, you miss out on what your partner is saying in the meantime. Just focus on what they have to say!

Remember that active listening, like anything else, is a skill—one that takes practice. Do not give up if you do not get it right the first time.

Create a Neutral Space

It can be hard to have a conducive conversation when you feel overpowered from the start, and usually, this can happen due to biased spaces. For example, if your partner has a den, home office, or other area specifically for them, having a conversation there can already feel like they are winning simply due to the fact that you are in their domain, so to speak.

Rather than conversing or arguing in biased spaces, find or create a neutral space to talk in. The living room is usually my favorite option for this. There is no bed to turn to for comfort and avoid the conversation, nor are there overly personal ties to one specific person. It is a neutral space where both parties feel like they are standing on equal ground.

Do Not Interrupt

It can be tempting to interrupt your partner, especially if you have something in mind that feels urgent to say. No point that you can make is worth interrupting your partner with such a show of disrespect. If you think of something dire to say, just wait until they have finished talking. And in the case that you do accidentally interrupt, a curt apology and a simple "What were you saying before I interrupted?" can right that wrong.

Be Honest

It might be tempting to cover up how you feel and save face, especially when talking to your partner; however, in order for your needs to be met and for you to be satisfied in your relationships it is important to be honest. Honesty does not mean being mean or rude, so be kind in how you honestly express what you are feeling and thinking. You'll notice that your needs are met far easier when you do.

Communication is a hard muscle to build, but with the above tools and your dedication, you'll notice marked improvements in the quality of your communication in no time! Now, let's move to a different realm of communication: problem-solving, and see how other tactics and techniques can improve your relationship!

Problem-Solving Tactics

Something else that you can do to improve your attachment and help resolve conflict within relationships is to work on your problem-solving skills. Conflict is inevitable, and a common misconception about conflict is that it's always bad. That's not the case at all! Conflict resolution and solving problems can actually strengthen a relationship, and that's what we're going to work on with these tactics.

Avoid Placing Blame

One thing that, without a doubt, escalates conflict is pointing fingers and placing blame. Even if you feel like something is 100% your partner's fault, don't be quick to place that blame on them. Nine times out of ten, they didn't really have the intention of hurting you or sabotaging the relationship. Even if a partner did something and it's their fault, it's not your place to point fingers; it is *their* responsibility to own up for what they did.

Instead of blaming one another in the face of a conflict, replace that blame with "I" statements. Try starting your sentences with words like "I feel" or "I think." This can be a responsible way to frame things from your perspective without placing blame and escalating the conflict.

Listen to Understand, Not to Respond

We talked about this in the last section, but make sure that you're listening with the intention of understanding your partner, and not with the intention of just saying something in response. When we listen to understand, conflicts are resolved faster; this allows you both to understand where each other is coming from more effectively.

Be Open-Minded

When you're in the middle of a conflict, it's important to be open-minded when it comes to solutions and what your partner has to say. Your partner might have suggestions that can resolve the conflict—ones that you didn't even think of. By remaining open-minded, you can collaborate on resolutions to any conflict that comes your way. Furthermore, your partner may have seemingly strange needs or desires, accommodations that make them more comfortable within the relationship. When you are open-minded to the needs of others, you don't have to worry about neglecting the needs of your partner because they asked for something unfamiliar to you.

Remain Calm

When you're in the middle of a conflict, one of the best things that you can do is try to remain calm. Oftentimes, one can get heated when a conflict is actively occurring; however, these heightened emotions for one or both parties don't resolve anything. High levels of emotions are linked to instigation, hostility, and passive aggression rather than conflict solution, meaning that it's always better to remain calm.

Of course, you can't necessarily force yourself to be calm in the middle of a pressing conflict. Don't be afraid to take a step back and ask for a break from the conversation to compose yourself or collect your thoughts, and then return to the conversation when you're feeling more at ease.

Validate Feelings

When resolving a conflict, your partner is probably being very vulnerable when they share their thoughts and feelings. You can help establish a secure connection and a resolution-focused mentality by being sure to validate their feelings. Some ways you can validate the feelings of your partner are through statements like

- I think I know what you mean.
- I feel the same way.
- I've experienced something like that before.

Then, if you have a proposed solution, don't force it onto them. Ask if they're open to hearing what you think would be a good way to solve the problem, and chances are, a resolution will come up on its own.

It's Not About Winning

Remember that the point of conflict resolution isn't to win or be "right." Rather, the point is to come to a compromise or agreeable solution that makes everyone happy. When arguing, it can be easy to try to assert yourself as right. If this happens, take a step back and realize that the greater purpose of the conversation is to help both of you be secure and happy—not to win a fight.

Now, you have some powerful skills that will enable you to overcome your problems within relationships, resulting in a happier, healthier, and stronger relationship. How amazing is that?

Nurturing Secure Attachment

We have talked a lot about communication and conflict resolution in the face of nurturing secure attachment, but what about other ways to ensure secure connection? In this section, you'll find some final ways to help you really nurture secure attachment in your life.

First, it is important that you take some time to truly and genuinely cultivate secure and supportive relationships. When you have lived your entire life with an insecure form of attachment, it is easy to find yourself surrounded by unsupportive individuals, haphazardly formed relationships, and other connections that are not conducive to your growth within a secure attachment style. Rather than trying to "fix" these relationships, make it a point to seek and form secure forms of attachment with supportive people—individuals who support your dreams, goals, and desires. This will help you attach more securely without a shadow of a doubt.

Boundary setting is vital for nurturing secure attachment as well. People with insecure attachment styles are not as likely to set strong boundaries; instead, they will allow people to walk on top of their boundaries or not set boundaries at all, resulting in poor treatment within the relationship. As such, it is important not only to set boundaries that accurately reflect what you need but you also have to be able to *communicate* those boundaries clearly as well—and stand up for yourself if and when someone crosses them.

Furthermore, it is vital for you to reflect on attachment patterns in your relationship. Think about the attachment style you have, as well as the attachment style of your partner. Considering how these styles of attachment impact a relationship overall is a wonderful way to foster secure attachment, as this fosters self-awareness when it comes to attachment-based conflict. Moreover, you should aim to understand and address insecure patterns as you have been doing. Even if you transition to a healthy style of attachment, it is important to regularly reflect and ensure that you are not subconsciously sinking back into poor attachment habits.

Finally, as we have talked about before, self-compassion is crucial to overcoming an insecure style of attachment. When you are unkind or harsh toward yourself, it makes it much harder to grow, change, and transform your style of attachment. On the other hand, if you have a mentality of compassion that you extend toward yourself, then you are much more likely to experience happiness and success when it comes to changing your attachment style.

Nurturing Emotional Regulation

Emotional regulation also has a lot to do with nurturing secure attachment, which is why we simply cannot avoid talking about it. When you can regulate your emotions, you can talk to and interact with others in a way that allows the two of you to have a stronger partnership. So, what can you do to foster true emotional regulation?

One way that you can work on emotional regulation skills tied to your style of attachment is through mindfulness. Mindfulness exercises like meditation, deep breathing, and yoga can promote better emotional responses due to the fact that you are anchored to the here and now. This means that when you have to have a challenging conversation or resolve conflict, you will be in a better headspace and have a better capacity to do so.

Furthermore, healthy lifestyle choices are known to contribute to overall higher emotional regulation skills. Making simple yet effective changes to the way you sleep, eat, and exercise can balance neurotransmitters and other neurochemicals for a healthier interaction with one's emotions. In fact, the mind-body connection is a well-established concept, and it ties deeply to emotional regulation. This means that your physical well-being does play a significant role in your ability to manage and regulate emotions.

Journaling is another way that you can work to harness true emotional regulation. When you feel a strong emotion or like you want to explode with emotions, just write it down. This helps you express your emotions without the negative impact that your emotions can have on those around you. An added benefit of journaling—which you can do with or without the help of prompts—is that you are able to find structure within your thoughts that allows you to communicate them more effectively.

Also, stress management techniques can really up the game when it comes to your emotional regulation skills. You can learn methods like progressive muscle relaxation, breathing tools, and more to help you deal with stress, anxiety, and other strong emotions that can interfere with your ability to manage and regulate your emotions.

If you struggle with regulating emotions on a deeper level, it can be a good idea to consider therapy or counseling. Within these areas, you can explore and manage emotions with valuable and professional tools for emotional regulation. There is no shame in seeking therapy or counseling; those tools are there for a reason, so make use of them!

Secure attachment is undoubtedly the way to go when it comes to relationships. The only relationships that are truly happy and healthy involve securely attached partners. And now, with everything you have learned, you can become one of those securely attached individuals, ensuring that your current and future relationships shine brighter than ever.

Conclusion

The dawn sets on a wonderful day of productivity and achievement, and you have the evening all to yourself. Now, with your newfound skills and strategies, you can enjoy that evening in a healthy manner—one that is filled with love, security, and vibrance.

Rather than anxiously awaiting a text back or shoving everyone away, now, you can curl up next to a partner who you know loves you, accepting basic strides of affection as you do. You're not worried about the "what if" questions that used to linger in your mind, nor do you feel as though control is slipping through your fingers.

That same night, you tuck into bed and feel relieved. Even if you occasionally have a worry pop up, you know how to handle it. You rest your eyes and go to sleep knowing that never again will attachment issues be the biggest barrier to your happiness. You are free to be unequivocally you, loving and being loved like you deserve.

This is the exact future that awaits you now that you've harnessed the power of what it means to have secure attachment. And similar benefits await in all tracks of your life—attachment isn't just about romance, and once you develop a secure attachment, healing in all areas of life follows.

Throughout the course of this book, you've confronted your attachment style head-on and learned every one of the best solutions to your particular woes. And as a result, your relationships will never be better.

As you continue to navigate your journey of attachment, remember that recovery isn't a linear process; some days are going to look like anxiety, overwhelm, and uncertainty. On those days, remember your goal. Remember that healthy attachment means working on yourself day in and day out, and those "bad" days are all a part of the process.

You have everything you need to get moving on this journey to healthy attachment. As someone who once stood where you are today, I know how harrowing the winding road of recovery can be. But if I did it, and if so many others did it, then you can do it too.

If you enjoyed this book and found the tools you picked up to be useful, please leave a review! Not only does this help me improve my work and resources for others, but your reviews allow people just like you to find these invaluable tools to kickstart their own recovery. With a click of a button, you can make an indelible impact!

To submit a review, kindly navigate to your Amazon Order History, locate the book in your purchased items, and select 'Write a Product Review.' If you are in the United States, you can also use the QR code provided below.

Outside of that, I highly recommend visiting my website, JoyceTbooks.com with Access Code **secure**. Not only are affirmations included, but a bonus workbook brimming with activities can be downloaded there as well.

Ready to transform your relationships? Start today. Take the first step toward lasting love and secure, and healthier, more fulfilling connections. You have everything it takes.

Bonus Gift

As a modest gesture to express my gratitude, I'm offering you a complimentary gifts that will play vital role in enhancing your success with this book:

Attachment Styles: Workbook (full e-Book) &
50 Affirmations for Anxiously Attached People(PDF file)

Scan QR code to download with Access Code: **secure**

www.JoyceTbooks.com

References

A guide to productively communicating your feelings (2019, February 13). Psych Company. https://www.psychcompany.com/productively-communicating-your-feelings/

admin. (2022, January 25). *Strategies for reframing negative thoughts.* St. Bonaventure University. https://online.sbu.edu/news/strategies-reframing-negative-thoughts

Anthony, R. (n.d.). *Robert Anthony quotes.* LinkedIn. https://www.linkedin.com/pulse/you-can-have-anything-want-willing-give-up-belief-cant-gudkov/

Attachment styles and how they affect relationships. (n.d.). Help Guide. https://www.helpguide.org/articles/relationships-communication/attachment-and-adult-relationships.htm#:~:text=Disorganized%20attachment-

Brennan, D. (2021, April 8). *What is anxious attachment?* WebMD. https://www.webmd.com/mental-health/what-is-anxious-attachment

Carapeto, M. J., & Veiga, G. (2023). Emotional awareness mediates the relationship between attachment and anxiety symptoms in adolescents. *Mental Health & Prevention,* 200269. https://doi.org/10.1016/j.mhp.2023.200269

Cherry, K. (2023, February 22). *What is attachment theory?* Verywell Mind. https://www.verywellmind.com/what-is-attachment-theory-2795337

Dreisoerner, A., Junker, N. M., & van Dick, R. (2021). The relationship among the components of self-compassion: A pilot study using a compassionate writing intervention to enhance self-kindness, common humanity, and mindfulness. *Journal of Happiness Studies, 22*(1), 21–47. https://doi.org/10.1007/s10902-019-00217-4

Fraley, C. (2018). *A brief overview of adult attachment theory and research.* R. Chris Fraley.

http://labs.psychology.illinois.edu/~rcfraley/attachment.htm

Ford, D. (n.d.). *Debbie Ford quotes.* BrainyQuotes. https://www.brainyquote.com/quotes/debbie_ford_712256#:~:text=Debbie%20Ford%20Quotes&text=Self%2Dawareness%20is%20the%20ability%20to%20take%20an%20honest%20look,or%20wrong%2C%20good%20or%20bad.

Graebner, K. (2021, June 18). *How to practice self compassion and tame your inner critic.* Better up. https://www.betterup.com/blog/self-compassion

Greenblatt, L. (n.d.). *How to meditate: A step-by-step guide.* Lion's Roar. https://www.lionsroar.com/how-to-meditate/

Hamarta, E., Engin Deniz, M., & Saltali, N. (2009). *Attachment styles as a predictor of emotional intelligence.* https://files.eric.ed.gov/fulltext/EJ837780.pdf

Harvard Health Publishing. (2021, February 12). *4 ways to boost your self-compassion.* Harvard Health.

https://www.health.harvard.edu/mental-health/4-ways-to-boost-your-self-compassion

Holmes, J. (n.d.). *Attachment theory.* Thrive Treatment. https://thrivetreatment.com/attachment-theory/

Maraboli, S. (n.d.). *Renew yourself.* Motivating Daily. https://motivatingdaily.com/2019/11/

How a disorganized attachment style impacts relationships and how to heal. (2023, June 20). Verywell Mind. https://www.verywellmind.com/disorganized-attachment-in-relationships-7500701

How attachment styles affect adult relationships. (n.d.). HelpGuide.org https://www.helpguide.org/articles/relationships-communication/attachment-and-adult-relationships.htm#:~:text=Disorganized%2Fdisoriented%20attachment%2C%20also%20referred

How to fix an anxious attachment style. (2022, December 6). Medical News Today. https://www.medicalnewstoday.com/articles/how-to-fix-anxious-attachment-style#:~:text=An%20anxious%20attachment%20style%20is%20usually%20the%20result%20of%20feelings

How to heal avoidant attachment style. (n.d.). Liberation Healing Seattle. https://www.liberationhealingseattle.com/blog-trauma-therapist/how-to-heal-avoidant-attachment-style

How to heal avoidant attachment style: A guide. (2023, March 5). https://veritaspsychotherapy.ca/blog/how-to-heal-avoidant-attachment/

How to meditate. (2019, April 13). Mindful. https://www.mindful.org/how-to-meditate/

Huang, S. (2020, August 24). *Attachment styles.* Simply Psychology. https://www.simplypsychology.org/attachment-styles.html

Learning about thought reframing. (n.d.). MyHealth. https://myhealth.alberta.ca/Health/aftercareinformation/pages/conditions.aspx?hwid=abk7438

Litchfield, B. (2022, February 15). *7 tips for anxious attachment styles in a relationship*. The Couples Center. https://www.thecouplescenter.org/7-tips-for-anxious-attachment-styles-in-a-relationship/

Manson, M. (2021, January 13). *Attachment theory*. Mark Manson. https://markmanson.net/attachment-styles

Martin, S. (2017, January 20). *How to communicate your feelings*. Psych Central. https://psychcentral.com/blog/imperfect/2017/01/how-to-communicate-your-feelings

Neff, K. D. (2009). The role of self-compassion in development: A healthier way to relate to oneself. *Human Development, 52*(4), 211–214. https://doi.org/10.1159/000215071

NHS. (2022, September 26). *Reframing unhelpful thoughts—self-help CBT techniques—every mind matters*. NHS. https://www.nhs.uk/every-mind-matters/mental-wellbeing-tips/self-help-cbt-techniques/reframing-unhelpful-thoughts/

Psychology Today. (2019). *Attachment*. Psychology Today.

https://www.psychologytoday.com/us/basics/attachment

Rehabilitation, B. (2022, January 25). *How To overcome your negative core beliefs*. The Beachcomber Rehabilitation.

https://thebeachcomberrehabilitation.com/blog/how-to-overcome-your-negative-core-beliefs/

Relationships—creating intimacy. (2021). Better Health

https://www.betterhealth.vic.gov.au/health/HealthyLiving/relationships-creating-intimacy

Smith, A. (2020, November 12). *Avoidant attachment: Symptoms, signs, causes, and more*. Medical News Todayhttps://www.medicalnewstoday.com/articles/avoidant-attachment

Some ways to resolve conflicts. (n.d.). Clackamas County. https://www.clackamas.us/ccrs/resolve.html

Strengthen your relationships with attachment exercises. (2021, January 26). Amanda Ann Gregory. https://www.amandaanngregory.com/strengthen-your-relationships-with-attachment-exercises

Team. (2023, January 2). *Emotional intelligence and attachment.* Attachment Project. https://www.attachmentproject.com/blog/emotional-intelligence-attachment/

10 Powerful journal prompts for healing avoidant attachment. (2023, June 14). Selebriti.cloud. https://selebriti.cloud/en/journal-prompts-for-avoidant-attachment/

The Attachment Project. (2020a, July 2). *Anxious attachment: Causes & symptoms.* Attachment Project. https://www.attachmentproject.com/blog/anxious-attachment/

The Attachment Project. (2020b, July 2). *Avoidant attachment style—learn the causes and symptoms.* Attachment Project.

https://www.attachmentproject.com/blog/avoidant-attachment-style/

Think someone has an avoidant attachment style? Here's how to tell. (2023, May 24). Mindbodygreen. https://www.mindbodygreen.com/articles/avoidant-attachment

Printed in Great Britain
by Amazon